BOWLING FOR EVERYONE

*the text of this book is printed
on 100% recycled paper*

BOWLING FOR EVERYONE

GENE BERGER
with Nancy Bogen

Photographs by Robert E. DiMilia
Line drawings & diagrams by Emmett McConnell

BARNES & NOBLE BOOKS
A DIVISION OF HARPER & ROW, PUBLISHERS
New York, Hagerstown, San Francisco, London

*This book is dedicated to my daughters,
Marcia, Anita, Valerie, and Laura,
and my good friend,
George Warshaw.*

This book is published in hardcover by St. Martin's Press. It is here reprinted by arrangement.

BOWLING FOR EVERYONE. Copyright © 1973 by Gene Berger. All rights reserved. Printed in the United States of America. No part of this book may be used or reproduced in any manner without written permission except in the case of brief quotations embodied in critical articles and reviews. For information address St. Martin's Press, 175 Fifth Avenue, New York, N.Y. 10010. Published simultaneously in Canada by Fitzhenry & Whiteside Limited, Toronto.

First BARNES & NOBLE BOOKS edition published 1974.

STANDARD BOOK NUMBER: 06–463419–1

77 78 79 80   12 11 10 9 8 7 6 5 4 3

CONTENTS

Introduction 7

1 ALL ABOUT THE GAME 9
2 THE PROPER EQUIPMENT 21
3 FROM THE RETURN RACK TO THE FOUL LINE 31
4 STRIKES AND SPARES 62
5 "PROBLEM" BOWLERS 89
6 BOWLING ETIQUETTE 112
7 BOWLING FAULTS AND HOW TO CORRECT THEM 114

Glossary 128
Appendix: ABC General Playing Rules 136

ACKNOWLEDGEMENTS

I wish to express my thanks for the co-operation of Roy Moscowitz, Allen Wesslock, Mary Benaducci, and Virginia DiMilia for their time as models, and Roy Kurre of Hill Lanes in Madison, New Jersey and Michael La Morte of Colonial Lanes, Staten Island for the use of their facilities. The late Joe Falcaro I shall always remember for his kind encouragement and suggestions; I want to thank Joe Jr., Al Fuscarino, Joe Cirillo, and ABC's Joe Adessa for the same.

INTRODUCTION

If you've always wanted to bowl but never tried it or once did and would like to again, this book is for you. For in my opinion, bowling is simplicity itself. Anyone can learn how to do it—and with finesse too!

What does it take? Really not very much. The ability to learn, which as a human you have, and a little time and patience, which if you don't have, you can easily acquire.

In this book a prospective amateur bowler will find all

that he needs to know about bowling, including the basic rules of the game, scoring, equipment, basic techniques, bowling etiquette, and common faults and their corrections. One unique feature is the attention I give to "problem" bowlers, like the left-handed, women, and the handicapped.

You may well ask what my particular claim to fame is. After all, I am virtually unknown in the professional bowling world. How can I set myself up as an authority? The truth of the matter is that I am a pro, but a teaching rather than a playing one. I have had many years of experience as an instructor on the lanes and consequently I have had more than ample opportunity to observe others, pro's as well as amateurs. In other words, I know the game best from the bench, and I can say with confidence, so far as you the amateur are concerned, that I know the game best for you. All too often a playing pro, when writing about bowling, will overlook the possible differences between him and his readers, and suggest techniques or procedures that take expertise for granted. He fails to realize that his goals and your goals are not the same. Bowling is his livelihood; all you want to do is engage in a sport, get some exercise, and perhaps meet people like yourself. My instructions are geared to take the sting of inadequacy out of amateur bowling.

It is my sincere hope that this book is of benefit to you. By studying it attentively, following the instructions carefully, and practicing regularly, pretty soon you will

Push out—down—back—and—bowl
GENE BERGER

1
ALL ABOUT THE GAME

Basic Rules

The sport or game of bowling involves two or more players competing at the same time. Their object is simple: to send a large, heavy, hard-surface ball down a long lane of polished wood towards ten tenpins, and to cause as many of these pins to fall down as possible. Each player is entitled to ten turns per game, a turn (or *frame*, as it is called) consisting of at least one chance and at the most two chances to roll the ball. If your first roll is really devastating and you succeed in sending all of the pins sprawling, you have bowled a *strike*, and that is the end of your turn. If not, then you are entitled to another chance, this time at whatever pins your first roll left standing. These remaining pins are commonly known as a *spare leave*. If you knit brain and brawn together and manage to mow them down, then you have bowled what is called a *spare* (actually you have achieved a *spare conversion*). If you do not "convert the spare" then you are left with what is called an *open frame*. Bowling procedure is the same for each frame, except that if you score a strike with the first roll of your tenth and final turn, the pins are set up again and you are given two more chances to roll the ball. If you convert the spare in your final turn, the pins are reset and you are given one more roll.

Scoring

When two or more people bowl a game, they keep a record of their performance by frame on a *score sheet*. A strike is worth ten points plus the number of pins knocked down by the player's next two rolls. A spare counts for ten points plus the number of pins felled by the next roll. If the player fails either to achieve a strike or to convert the spare, his score for that frame is simply the total number of pins picked off by his two rolls. Each bowler's score is carried over cumulatively from frame to frame, and at the end of the tenth and last frame, the one with the highest score is the winner.

All About the Game

The actual recording of each bowler's performance from frame to frame is precise and exacting, so don't be surprised if it takes you a little while to master it. A score sheet is divided up into horizontal lines: one line per player per game. Each line begins at the left with a space for the player's name and continues with eleven boxes. The first ten are for your cumulative score frame by frame, the last for your grand total. The upper right-hand corner of the first nine of these boxes contains two little boxes, that of the tenth, three. These boxes are used to note what happens with each roll of the ball.

What can happen? Strike—spare—split—open frame—ball rolls into channel—complete miss—foul.

If you achieve a strike in a given frame, an "X" is placed in the first little box, and the second little box is left blank. If you convert a spare, the number of pins you felled with your first roll is set down in the first little box, and a "/" is placed in the second little box. Converted or not, if your spare is a *split*, that is, the second roll involves pins not standing next to one another, the number in the first little box is circled. For an open frame the number of pins you picked off with each of your rolls is marked down in the two little boxes. If your ball goes into one of the side channels without hitting anything, it is so indicated by a *C* in one (or both) of the little boxes. If for any other reason your ball fails to make contact with the pins, a "-" is used instead. There are fouls in bowling as in most other sports, and these likewise involve a penalty. If you commit a foul on a given occasion, an *F* is marked down in the little box, and whatever points you racked up with that roll are forfeited.

BOWLING FOR EVERYONE

To illustrate, let's consider the sample score sheet line given below. In the first frame, the bowler, John Smith, knocked down seven pins with his first ball and went on to convert the spare with his second. He wasn't so skillful in the second or third frame, knocking down only nine pins in each and failing to get any with his second ball in the third frame. The fourth frame was his best—he made a strike. And the fifth frame wasn't so bad either, when he knocked down eight pins with his first ball and converted the spare. But the next four frames were trouble again. In the sixth frame, after dropping nine pins with his first ball, he sent his second ball into one of the channels. In the seventh and then again in the ninth frame, his first ball left a split, and only in the latter was he able to convert the spare. The eighth frame was a disaster: he lost the points he made with his first ball by committing a foul. John rallied somewhat in the last frame, scoring a strike again, but he was unable to do more than hit six and three pins with his remaining two balls.

Name	1	2	3	4	5	6	7	8	9	10	Total
John	7 / 18	8 1 27	9 - 36	X 56	8 / 75	9 C 84	⑨ 1 93	F 8 101	⑨ / 121	X 6 3 140	140

Score sheet.

Beginning and Developing

The highest possible score that can be made in bowling is 300, and this requires knocking off twelve strikes in a row. But never fear, such perfection is seldom achieved on the lanes, even by champions—though most of those fellows average well over 200. If you have never bowled before or are going to take it up again after a considerable lapse of time, expect scores below 125 and even 100. After three or four months of diligent practice, you should score between 125 and 150. Further practice coupled with playing experience should result in scores between 150 and 200. It is best, especially if you are unaccustomed to exercising regularly, to begin practicing gradually, mastering the fundamentals outlined in this book, then going on to bowl three lines (or games) one day a week and later, a number of times a week. Do this alone, or with a member of your family, or with a friend who is also beginning or starting afresh—and keep a record of your scores so you have an indication of your progress. Learning with someone can be fun and, if nothing else, it will whet your appetite for real competition.

Competitive Bowling

Once you begin racking up scores of 125 to 150, you should think about formally competing with others. The best way to do this is to join a team or form one. Teams are organized by league, and your local bowling center is probably the home of a variety of them. Take your pick: there are five-, four-, three-, two-, and even one-man team leagues. There are leagues for average (130-160), better-than-average (160-190), champion (over 200), and even beginning (under 125) bowlers. And then there are commercial leagues: those sponsored by some business,

BOWLING FOR EVERYONE

industry, union, fraternal organization, or religious group. Most of these leagues are members of the American Bowling Congress (*ABC*). The ABC, in addition to sponsoring and promoting national tournaments (which you may wish to observe and even participate in), also sets league rules and regulations (see Appendix) and conducts a regular inspection of bowling facilities to insure some degree of uniformity.

In the eastern and midwestern parts of the United States, the bowling league season runs from right after Labor Day to the beginning of May, with summer leagues taking over after that. In the south and west, regular league bowling lasts straight through the year. Most leagues bowl once a week at a regular hour. The usual procedure is for each team of a league to play a *match* (three games or lines) with every other team. In a given round, the team with the greatest number of matches to its credit is the winner.

When you feel you've had enough of practicing and crave a little action, inquire at your local bowling center about the kinds of leagues that use its facilities and fill out application forms for the ones that seem most suited to you. Sometime before the season begins, these leagues will hold general meetings at which you may petition for membership for yourself or your team. Then, once you have been accepted, the real fun begins.

Even after being accepted into a league, you will have to continue practicing a couple of hours a week if you want to maintain your average. This *average*, by the way, is arrived at by considering your first three matches (or nine

All About the Game

games) of league play in a given season. The figure is sent to the ABC by your league secretary or team captain and kept on file there as your official average for the season.

The Bowling Center

A bowling center nowadays is just that: an all-purpose "center" which usually contains a restaurant, a bar, seat-

Modern bowling center.

ing areas for spectators, meeting rooms, and a nursery—as well as bowling areas and a pro shop where you can buy bowling equipment. A bowling area consists of a lane with two channels, one on either side, an area at one end of the lane, called the *approach*, and an area at the other end of the lane, called the *pindeck*. In a given center there may be as few as six bowling areas and as many as a hundred or more.

By ABC regulation, the lane proper may be forty-one to forty-two inches wide and measure sixty feet from one extremity to the other, that is from the *foul line*, which separates it from the approach, to the center of the first pin (number 1 or *head pin*) of the pindeck. By ABC regulation also, the lane must consist of thirty-nine to forty-two boards of either maple or pine and be finished with lacquer or shellac. A couple of decades ago, shellacked pine was popular, but today owners of bowling centers favor lacquered maple. No matter what the nature of the wood and finish—lacquered maple, shellacked pine, shellacked maple, lacquered pine—the surface is always polished with oil, the amount used varying from center to center. A lane may have one or two sets of markings, but there is no rule requiring that it have any markings at all. Allowable is either 1) a set of ten circular figures set six to eight feet beyond the foul line or 2) a set of seven angular figures set twelve to sixteen feet beyond the foul line. Observe these markings well, as they may prove important should you choose to learn *spot bowling*, a particular method of aiming the ball (covered in Chapter 4 under *Aiming Your Ball*).

All About the Game

The channels on either side of a lane are a little over nine inches wide. They are placed there to prevent your ball from rolling onto an adjacent lane should it suddenly veer off course.

The approach is fifteen feet long and is of course the same width as the lane—forty-one to forty-two inches. It may be made of wood or granite; usually it is of pine. As with lanes, the approach may also have a number of markings, but again there is no rule requiring these markings. Allowable are one, two, or as many as three rows of seven circular figures, these to be located respectively two to six inches, eleven to twelve feet, and fourteen to fifteen feet behind the foul line. These markings may be useful as aids in determining where to stand with your ball before taking aim (see Chapter 3, *Step B: Assuming a Stance on the Approach*). Since any spilled liquid or food in this approach area may have a bad effect on your game and can even cause serious injury, make it a rule of thumb never to bring any beverages or snacks there, and before bowling, be sure that it has been left clean and dry by the previous bowler. It might not even be a bad idea to take a few practice steps and slides.

Close by the approach are usually a settee for waiting between frames and a lighted desk for score-keeping. Ultra-modern bowling centers provide each desk with an automatic scoring device as an aid toward more consistent and accurate score-keeping. This device notes when a pin has been knocked down by the pinsetting machine rather than by your ball, and can provide a printed record of your pinfall roll by roll.

BOWLING FOR EVERYONE

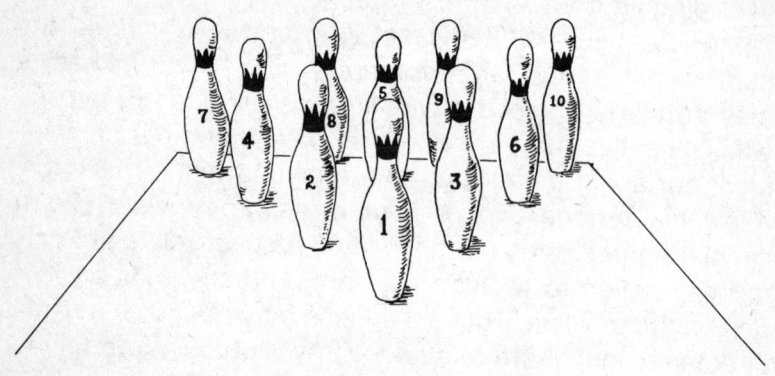

The pindeck.

The pindeck measures 34-3/16 inches from the center of the 1-pin to a panel (called the *tail plank*) behind the last row of pins. It is, of course, the same width as the lane and the approach. The pins are arranged in four rows in the form of a triangle: the 1-pin on the first row, the 2- and 3-pins on the second, the 4-, 5-, and 6-pins on the third, and the 7-, 8-, 9-, and 10-pins on the fourth. The centers of the spots on which the pins stand are 12 inches apart and equidistant from one another.

The pins themselves are each 15 inches high, 4-1/2 inches in diameter at their broadest section, and weigh

All About the Game   19

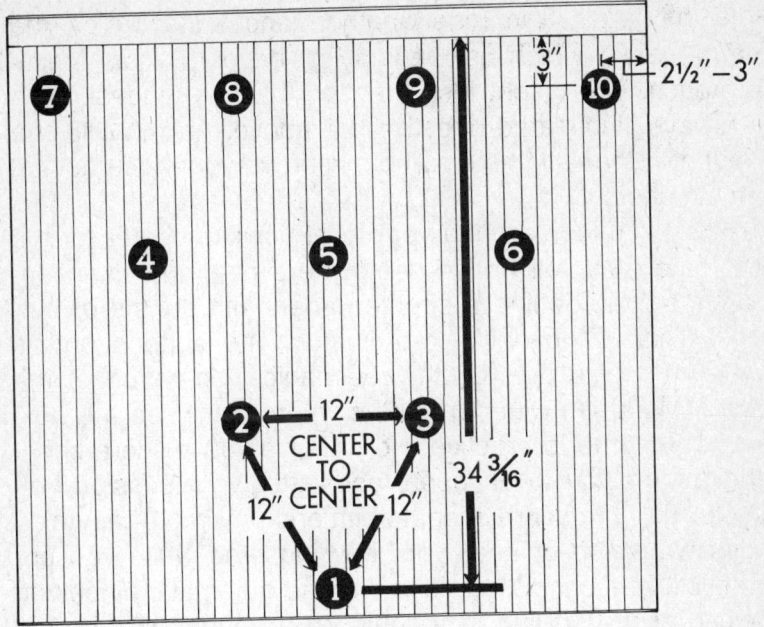

The pindeck from overhead, showing position and distance between pins.

between three pounds three ounces and three pounds ten ounces—all this by ABC regulation. Their top parts are generally made of maple, their bases plastic or nylon, and they are coated all over with a plastic finish.

Most bowling centers feature an *automatic pinsetting device* in each pindeck area. This machine sweeps away any pins knocked down by your first roll, resets the pindeck after you finish a frame, and sends your ball back to you after each roll. The ball moves along the *ball return*, a channel located between the two channels that separate adjacent lanes from one another, and ends up on the *return rack*, which is behind or beyond your area's approach. One might also mention that the pindeck area is always illuminated directly from above. As you will see presently, these lights may help improve your accuracy on certain shots.

When you look around your local bowling center for the first time, you will notice somewhere near the main entrance a man behind a counter laden with panels of buttons. This is the desk co-ordinator. The buttons on his panels have to do with the mechanical operation of the lanes. Mark him well, for it is he whom you'll see the next time you come to practice. He will give you a score sheet and assign you to an open lane; after your session you will turn in your score sheet to him and pay him. If anything goes wrong on or near your bowling area while you are practicing,—such as the failure of the automatic pinsetting device or the spilling of a liquid on an approach—he will take care of the matter when you call on him. The desk co-ordinator is also generally a mine of information about leagues using the center, and can refer you to a pro for private instruction if you feel you need it.

2
THE PROPER EQUIPMENT

Just as with every other sport, so with bowling, you will find that certain pieces of equipment are indispensable and others, which may seem indispensable, are not. You, of course, must be the final judge. But before making any decisions, do consider my suggestions, which are based not only on many years of experience as a teacher of bowling, but also time spent on the sidelines as a critical observer of the pro's.

BOWLING FOR EVERYONE

The two pieces of bowling equipment that *are* indispensable—a bowling ball and bowling shoes—may at first be acquired on a temporary basis at your bowling center. But before considering these items, let's dwell for a moment on a piece of equipment that is even more important.

Your Body

Anyone who wishes to bowl ought to be in good general health. This does not mean that you have to be a muscle man, but you should be able to indulge in a moderate amount of physical exercise without doing violence to your system, and your vision, with or without glasses, must be 20/20. If you have not engaged in anything resembling physical activity for a long period of time, it's best to start with a thorough medical check-up. Then, before even attempting to lift a bowling ball, undertake some mild form of body building. For this use any system of general exercises, like the *Royal Canadian Air Force Plans for Physical Fitness*.

Beyond the general exercises, a little time and effort should be spent on the further development of your shoulders, arms, hands, and legs, as these parts of the body are essential to effective bowling. Let me recommend what I myself do to keep fit. Begin by doing each of these exercises as many times as you can without tiring, counting to six with each change of position.

The Proper Equipment 23

1. *For the shoulders and arms*
    Stand up straight, make your arms taut, and lock your hands in front of your lap. Now slowly raise your arms until they are parallel with the floor. Finally, keeping the rest of your body immobile, swing your arms once to the left, once to the right, and then lower them to your starting position.

2. *For the arms and hands*
    Stand up straight with your arms at your sides, and make a fist with each hand, squeezing them as tight as you can. Now raise your arms in front of you until they are parallel with the floor. Finally, extend each to the side and lower them again, pulling down as hard as you can.

3. *For the legs*
    Lie flat on your back with your hands behind your head and raise your legs, keeping them taut and straight, three to four inches from the ground. Now spread them apart and bring them together again, finally lowering them to your starting position.

After your first few sessions, gradually try to increase the number of times you do these exercises. And by all means continue them—though perhaps not as frequently—after you have begun to bowl regularly.

If it turns out that you were born with weak shoulders, arms, hands, or legs and never did anything to remedy them, then I recommend that you try additional exercises beyond the above—chinning if you have underdeveloped shoulders and arms, squeezing a rubber ball if your hands are weak, and jogging if the problem is with your legs.

Your Bowling Ball

ABC regulation bowling balls are roughly twenty-six to twenty-seven inches in circumference and weigh from ten to sixteen pounds, those over twelve pounds being intended for adults. The heavier the ball you use the more effective your game will be, but it may be well to begin with a lighter one, say between twelve and fourteen pounds, and gradually progress to heavier ones as your skill improves. Of course, if you have no difficulty controlling a fifteen or sixteen pounder at first, by all means use it.

The ABC specifies that a ball be made of a nonmetallic material. Currently used are balls of hard rubber, plastic, and lucite. Your best bet, in my opinion, is a *rubber* one, as there is more friction between it and the high polish of a lane, and it is easier to control than one made of either of the other materials.

There is no rule as to the number of fingerholes in a ball; today one sees mostly two and three fingerholes around the lanes. I recommend a *three-holed ball*, since maneuvering a ball with three fingers seems to put less strain on the hand than with two and so the ball is easier to control. To grasp a ball with three holes, insert your thumb into the largest hole and your middle and ring fingers into the other two. When making a selection from among a number of three-holed balls, be certain that your thumb is comfortably loose in its hole—you should be able to rotate it in a circle—and your other fingers comfortably tight in theirs.

Another decision you will have to make concerns *span*, the distance between the thumbhole and the other two. And before deciding this you will have to decide on your grip, that is, how shallowly or how deeply you will insert your fingers in the holes, since the span will vary on the same ball depending on the grip. There are three grips in use on the lanes nowadays: the full conventional (all three fingers inserted up to the second joint), the full fingertip or full stretch (thumb inserted to the second joint, other fingers to the first joint), and the semi-fingertip or semi-conventional or semi-stretch (thumb inserted to the second joint, the other fingers to midway between the second and first joints). I recommend the semi-fingertip grip, as it puts less strain on the hand than the full fingertip grip, and is easier to pull your fingers out of than the full conventional. In my opinion it allows for the greatest amount of control.

After you have settled on a grip, you should perform a simple test to determine if the span of a particular ball is right for you: suspend the ball in the air by your fingers and observe the space between your palm and the ball. If the space is large enough to admit a thin pencil, the span is all right. But if the space is larger or there is hardly any space or no space at all, it is not.

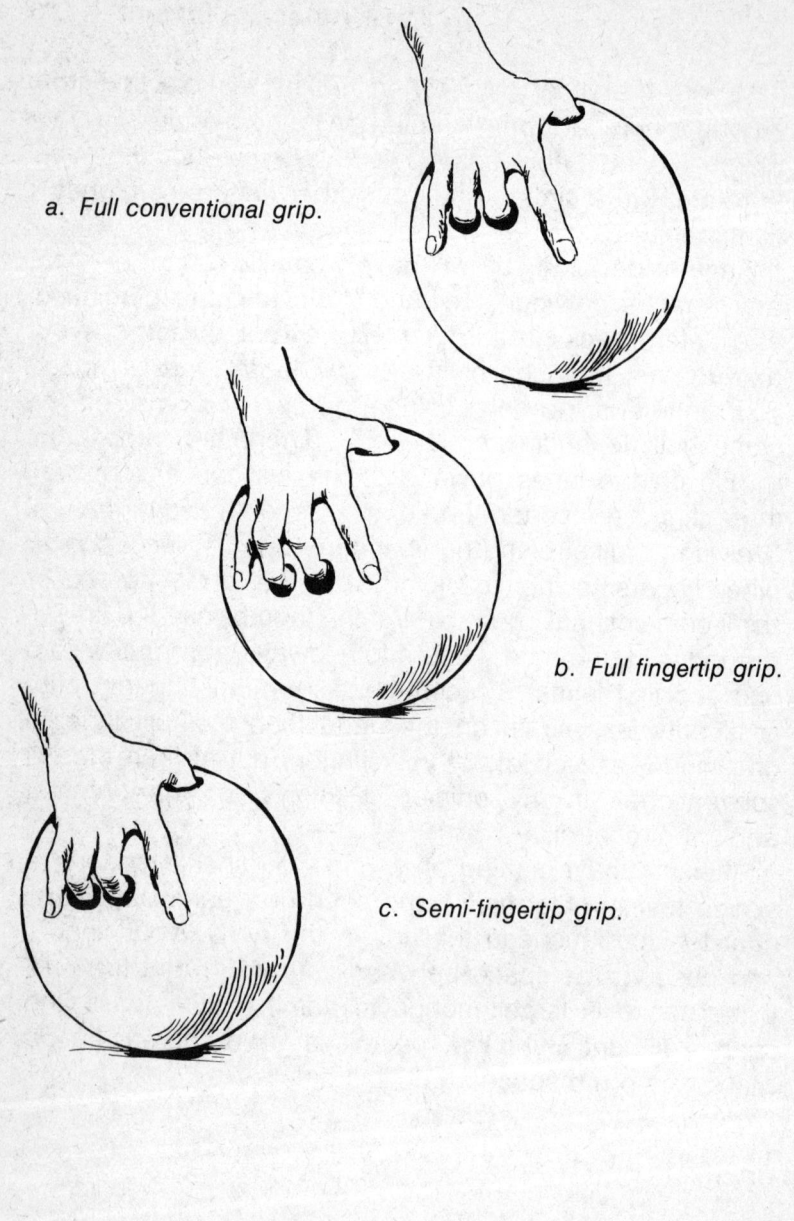

a. Full conventional grip.

b. Full fingertip grip.

c. Semi-fingertip grip.

The Proper Equipment 27

When you have chosen a ball based on considerations of weight, material of composition, the number of fingerholes, and span, take a trial swing with it, and even try rolling it down a lane once. If at any time you seem to lose control of it—if it seems to want to roll you down the lane—the ball is really not for you. Discard it and find another.

All that has been said up to now applies to *house balls*, that is, the balls that your bowling center provides free of charge for your use at a given session. These you will find on racks somewhere between the desk co-ordinator and the bowling areas. Usually there is a pretty fair selection.

House balls, however, are made for "average" hands, and you, being an individual with a unique pair of hands, will never find one that is a perfect fit. And so you should think about eventually acquiring your own ball, one with the precise weight you desire, and with the holes drilled for your bowling hand. When you have a ball drilled, you must take into consideration not only span but also the *bridge* (distance between middle and ring fingers), *offset* (difference in distance between thumb and middle finger and thumb and ring finger), and *pitch* (slant of the fingerholes in relation to the center). House balls are conventionally pitched, which means they are slanted toward the center, but your hand may require back pitch (the opposite of conventional pitch) or side pitch (slanted toward the palm). Most bowling center pro shops are staffed by a professional ball driller who can advise you further on this matter.

Bowling balls, in comparison to say baseball gloves,

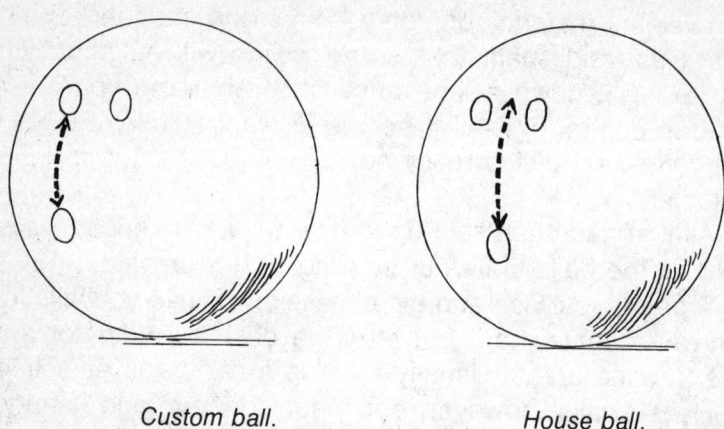

Custom ball. *House ball.*

require a minimum of care, but for a consistently effective game you ought to attend to that minimum regularly. Because bowling lanes are frequently oiled, your ball is bound to pick up not only a surface slick of oil but also dust and other foreign matter. And so it is a good idea to bring a piece of cloth with you to the bowling center and wipe off your ball now and then. Periodically your ball should be washed down with a liquid cleaner made for that purpose and available at the pro shop or a sporting goods store. This you can do at home with a piece of burlap, or have your bowling center do it—many have power-driven machines for the job. Also from time to time, inspect your ball for chipped fingerholes and have these promptly repaired or, if the damage is extensive, plugged and the ball redrilled.

The Proper Equipment

Your Bowling Shoes

Wearing shoes that are especially designed for bowling is as important as using a ball whose weight and fingerholes are suited to you. And so regard this as a golden rule of bowling: never wear street shoes or sneakers when bowling, not even the first time. The right sole of a bowling shoe is made of rubber, this to give you good traction; the left, of leather, for sliding. Both heels are of white rubber, so you will not make any ugly marks on the approach while in the process of rolling your ball. Sanitized bowling shoes in your size may be rented for a small charge at your bowling center, but as with the bowling ball, you should eventually think about acquiring your own. The pro shop of your bowling center probably has a selection from which you can choose. If you have particularly sensitive feet, consider buying or renting them a half size larger so they can accommodate an extra heavy pair of socks.

Whether your bowling shoes are rented or purchased, it is not a good idea to wander around in them: the soles may pick up gum or other foreign matter and ruin your performance the next time you bowl. Not to mention the danger to life and limb. If for some reason it is necessary for you to leave your bowling area with bowling shoes on, be sure to inspect them carefully before bowling again, and as a double check, why not take another trial slide on the approach as well.

Your Ball Bag

To avoid possible damage to your ball in transit, you

should carry it in some kind of container. If you do not have some kind of satchel for it at home, your pro shop probably does, and many ball bags have special compartments for bowling shoes.

Clothing

Unlike many other sports, there is no special uniform for bowling, so you may dress as you please. But I do recommend that your shirts be loose-fitting enough in the shoulders and armpits and your trousers in the waist and seat—but not so loose as to hinder the swinging or bending of your arm—to allow for maximum freedom of movement. Particularly comfortable are shirts with bi-swing backs or ribbed inserts or else knit shirts. All of these should be extra long and made of cotton, because of its absorbent quality. Trousers should have elastic waistbands.

Gadgets and Gloves

The ABC specifies that a ball must be bowled manually, so beware of ads that promise to do some or all of the job for you through special devices. The use of gloves is not prohibited, and there are a few bowling gloves on the market, but I do not recommend them unless you have extra sensitive hands. If this happens to be the case—and by all means remember this—*have your ball drilled or redrilled to fit your gloved hand.*

3
FROM THE RETURN RACK TO THE FOUL LINE

There are two moments of truth in bowling, the split second when your ball zips out of your hand and whizzes down the lane toward the pins and that other split second when it arrives. Let us concentrate on the first of these moments, leaving the other, which involves aiming, for the next chapter. Five steps are involved in this first moment of truth: conveying your ball from the return rack to the approach, delivering it to the foul line, releasing it, giving

32   BOWLING FOR EVERYONE

it direction and rotation, and following through. Let us consider each of these steps in turn.

Step A: Conveying Your Ball from the Return Rack to the Approach

When it's your turn to bowl, you will be expected to convey your ball from the return rack to the approach. The first thing you must learn is how to lift and carry your ball

Lifting the ball from return rack.

Holding ball in crook of elbow.

properly. This is done by turning your ball so that the thumbhole is close to your body and the other two fingerholes are away from it, raising your ball with a hand on either side, and placing it in the crook of your left elbow, which should be kept as close as possible to your left side. It should remain there until you are on the approach and ready to bowl. Never lift your ball in any other way; to do so is to risk injury to your arms and fingers and possibly your feet and toes should you accidentally drop it. It's especially important never to lift it with your fingers as that will put an undue strain on your hand and cause the fingerholes to become moist and slippery, thereby creating a real accident hazard.

Step B: Assuming a Stance on the Approach

Having learned how to lift and carry your ball properly, you're now ready to assume a stance on the approach in preparation for delivering the ball. To do this you must know how and where to place yourself on the approach.

There are two elements that determine your final position on the approach: distance from the foul line, and position between the two sides of the bowling lane or "sideways position." The first of these, distance from the foul line, will vary from lane to lane, but will remain constant for every shot bowled on the same lane. The second, sideways position, will vary from shot to shot, depending on your strategy for that particular shot.

Establishing your distance from the foul line and fixing

BOWLING FOR EVERYONE

it firmly in your mind is crucial. For if you begin your delivery too far from the foul line, your ball will have that much farther to travel and that much more opportunity to get into trouble. Or on the other hand, if you start your delivery too close and step on or cross the foul line while releasing your ball, you will have committed a foul. And that, as we have already noted, is a costly error. On the approach of a given lane your distance from the foul line will be the same for all shots, and this distance is fairly easy to establish. Pace off 4-1/2 normal walking steps from the foul line. Use this spot as a starting point. Now turn around and move straight ahead as follows: slide your right foot forward 1/2 step, take 2 normal walking steps, one with your left, the other with your right, and then take a long step with your left, ending it with a slide. This should bring you to about two inches from the foul line. If so, you have determined the proper distance from which you should start your delivery. If not—if you have reached or crossed the foul line or are considerably more than two inches behind it—then you must repeat the above procedure, starting either further back or closer in until you finally finish with that two-inch margin. Be sure to use the marks on the approach as guides to your starting points; that's what they're there for.

Unlike your distance from the foul line, your sideways position will vary with each shot. Determining it is bound up with aiming the ball. We'll cover this in the next chapter when we deal with aiming and individual shots. Suffice to say that for a strike delivery you stand in the center of the approach; for most spares, at different locations to the right or left of center.

Assuming stance.

36 BOWLING FOR EVERYONE

Once you have fixed both your distance from the foul line and sideways position, you are ready to assume your stance. Let us suppose, for the sake of demonstration, that your particular shot is a strike delivery. (In this case your sideways position is in the center of the approach; your distance from the foul line is standard, remember.) Check to be sure that your feet are parallel to the floor boards and two boards apart. Next move your right foot back so that its big toe is in line with the center of the instep of your left foot. Bend your knee slightly, at the same time tilting your head and trunk forward. Finally, shift the ball to your left hand, insert the proper fingers of your right hand into the fingerholes, and keeping your elbows close to your sides, raise and lower the ball with your left hand until you find a comfortable place between your chin and waist. This is the stance you should assume once you have determined your position on the approach: right foot parallel to but slightly behind your left foot, knees bent a little and body somewhat forward, left hand supporting your ball somewhere between chin and waist with the fingers of your right hand in the fingerholes.

Naturally, stances will vary from person to person, even among people of the same height and build. So do not be surprised or disturbed to find a guy on one side of you in a crouching position with his ball tucked under his chin and another guy on the other side of you standing almost erect with his ball down by his waist. Just do your own thing, making certain that your stance gives you a chance to be relaxed, balanced, and poised for action.

When settling into your stance, it is a good idea to

From the Return Rack

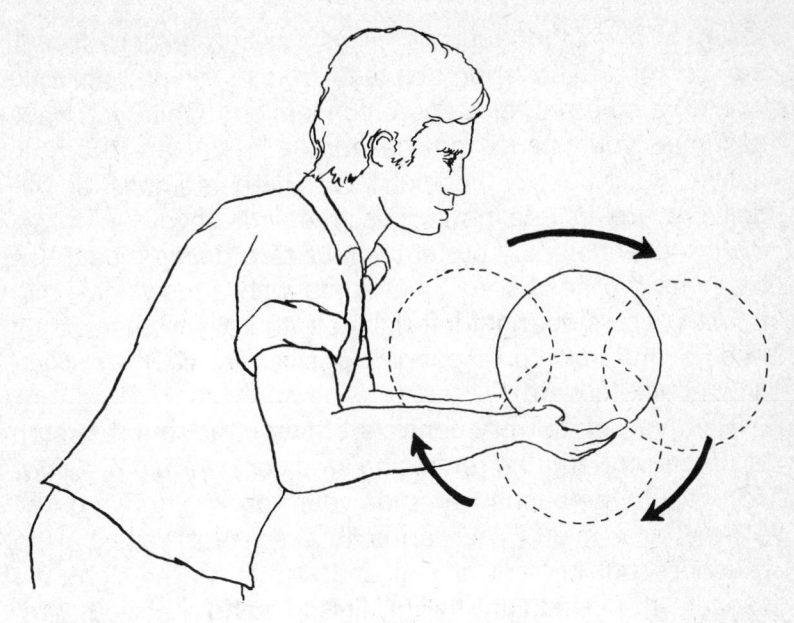

Waggling the ball.

"waggle" or heft your ball—just like the golfer who waggles his club before driving, the basketball player who bounces his ball before taking a foul shot, and the baseball player who takes a practice swing with his bat before a pitch. This helps ease tension—but beware of overdoing it. Too much waggling can produce the opposite effect.

Step C: Delivering Your Ball to the Foul Line

Let's continue to suppose you are bowling for a strike.

38 BOWLING FOR EVERYONE

(Keep in mind that your sideways position for this shot is the center of the approach and that in all probability it would be different for a spare conversion.) Once you have assumed your stance on the approach you are ready to deliver your ball to the foul line. Three methods of ball delivery are in use nowadays, methods involving three, four, and five steps. I prefer the *four-step delivery* because it seems the easiest to co-ordinate with armswings—that is, with each step (right-left-right-left) there is what appears to be a "natural" corresponding position for your arm (out-down-back-forward).

This type of delivery consists of two parts, the first step or *pushaway* and the remaining steps or *pendulum swing*. To execute the pushaway, slide your right foot forward half a step and make your arms taut so that your ball is "pushed" out in front of you and slightly to the right. To execute the pendulum swing, first imagine that your arm is attached to your shoulder by a hinge. Practice swinging your arm back and forth in a straight line like the pendulum of a grandfather's clock. With this motion fixed in your mind, remove your left hand from your ball, thrusting your left arm to the left for the sake of balance, and allow your ball to swing down while you take a normal walking step with your left foot, then allow it to swing back while you take another such step with your right foot. Finally, bring your ball forward and relax the grip of your thumb so that it "rolls off" your other fingers, at the same time taking a last step with your left foot, this one a little longer than the previous two and ending with a slide. As you do this, bend your left leg and tilt the upper part of your body forward. Thus while your left foot comes to a halt two inches before the foul line, your ball will leave your hand three or four inches beyond it. To insure that this happens, use your right foot as a brake; if this is not necessary, raise it slightly for the sake of balance.

If you execute this series of steps with armswings as directed, the end result will be as follows:

—Your left arm will be out to the left.
—Your left foot will be two inches from the foul line.
—Your left leg will be bent.
—Your shoulders will be ahead of your left knee.
—Your head will be ahead of your shoulders.
—Your right arm will be extended forward.
—Your right foot will be braking your left or raised slightly.

And, all other matters being equal, your roll will be an effective one.

Step D: Releasing Your Ball Toward the Pins

Just as there are different kinds of deliveries to the foul line, so too are there different ways of releasing your ball at the foul line. The most common are the straight ball, the hook ball, and the back-up ball releases. One way to distinguish among them is by the position of your hand on the ball.

Imagine, as you turn the ball in your bowling hand, that

First step pendulum swing: the pushaway.

Second step pendulum swing.

Third step pendulum swing.

Fourth step pendulum swing.

BOWLING FOR EVERYONE

a clockface has been superimposed upon it. This clockface remains stationary as you rotate the ball: six o'clock marks a perpendicular to the floor, twelve o'clock a perpendicular to the ceiling; three and nine o'clock mark perpendiculars to either wall. When you hold your ball so that your palm faces upward and a perpendicular from the center of the bridge intersects the twelve on your imaginary clockface, you're holding the ball in the twelve o'clock position. By turning the ball upside down (180 degrees) you reach the six o'clock position. The eleven-, ten-, nine-, one-, two-, three-o'clock positions describe gradations away from the twelve o'clock position.

The *straight ball release* results in a flat roll with no spin. It is comparable to a straight putt in golf. To execute this type of release, place your hand in the twelve o'clock position. The ball will proceed straight down the lane, skidding the first quarter of the way (about fifteen feet), then breaking into a roll for the remainder. The roll is produced by the upward action of your hand in the twelve o'clock position during the follow-through. This type of release is the easiest to learn and its results the most predictable. For these reasons I recommend your using it—but only after you are well versed in getting the ball from the return rack up to the foul line (Steps A through C). This type of release has a serious limitation: because a straight ball results in a flat roll without any spin, only the pins that it hits directly topple over; possibly—but just possibly—they will carry away the pins nearest them in their fall. This means that a straight ball must be aimed with pinpoint accuracy to knock down the pins you want to.

More sophisticated in knocking down pins and less taxing on your aiming ability is the *hook ball release*, which I recommend for all-around use once you have mastered your delivery and follow-through. This type of release results in a left hook or turn into the pindeck and a half-spin in a counter-clockwise direction. It is comparable to a billiard shot to the right or left of the center of the ball. To execute it, place your hand in the eleven o'clock position. The ball will proceed straight down the lane, skidding the first quarter of the way and breaking into a roll like the straight ball, but then, about two-thirds of the way down the lane (roughly forty feet), hooking to the left into the pindeck and picking up a semi-spinning motion or *english*. This hook to the left and semi-spin are produced by the upward action of your hand in the eleven o'clock position during the follow-through (see below). Together they make this type of release superior to the straight ball release, in that the ball, veering to the left and semi-spinning in roughly the same direction, can initiate chain reactions among the pins by causing them to spin among themselves as they fall. There is only one possible difficulty that may arise when you are executing the hook ball release: your wrist may turn or twist, thereby causing your ball to spin fully. A *full-spinner*, as you may soon learn to your dismay, is even less damaging in the pindeck area than a ball with no spin at all. To avoid this possibility, take care that your wrist remains straight from the beginning of the pushaway to the very end of the follow-through.

Once having learned to use this type of release to advantage, you can go on to a more commanding though

Hand position for straight ball.

Path of straight ball.

Hand position for hook ball.

Path of hook ball.

difficult version of it, one that will result in a *full roll* rather than a semi-spin. Place your hand in the twelve o'clock position for the first three steps of your delivery, then turn your wrist during the last step so that by the follow-through your hand is in the six o'clock position. The upward action of your hand in this position during the follow-through will produce the full roll, and a *full roller*, as you will soon see, is even more devastating in the pindeck area than a semi-spinner—but only with near-perfect control over the ball in other respects.

To be effective your hook ball ought to skid fifteen feet, roll twenty-five feet, and hook the remaining twenty feet. If your hook is longer, your ball has spent too much of its momentum, and if shorter then it hasn't gathered sufficient momentum, and in neither case will it cause any serious damage in the pindeck area. On most lanes—known as *normal* or *natural* lanes—you should have no difficulty in producing and maintaining the desired proportion of skid, roll, and hook. But on some lanes—called *fast* because your ball will not hook readily on it, or *slow* because it will do so all too readily—you will obviously have to make an adjustment in your delivery. Generally speaking, the kinds of materials used in the construction and maintenance of lanes and the weather account for variations. A surface of hard wood like maple, a hard finish like lacquer, a considerable amount of oil, and a dry atmosphere all contribute to making a lane fast; a surface of soft wood like pine, a soft finish like shellac, very little oil, and a humid atmosphere plus dust or other foreign matter all go into producing the opposite. Thus a lac-

From the Return Rack 51

quered maple lane will be faster than a shellacked one. Different amounts of oil may serve to equalize them, but on a dry day the lacquered lane will be faster than the shellacked one; on a wet day, slower.

To adjust your hook ball to a fast lane, do one or more of the following, depending upon the "fastness":

>1. *Slow down the speed of your ball* either by lowering it slightly at the top of the pushaway and thus shrinking the arc of your pendulum swing; or by decreasing your distance from the foul line, thereby forcing yourself to take smaller steps and slow down your delivery; or by releasing your ball in the nine or ten o'clock position.
>
>2. *Change the direction of your ball's course* by moving your sideways position slightly more to the right or left of where you would ordinarily assume it.
>
>3. *Decrease the amount of your ball's english* by moving your pinky closer to your ring finger and your index finger further away from your middle finger.

To adjust your hook ball to a slow lane, do one or more of the following, depending upon the "slowness":

>1. *Increase the speed of your ball* either by raising it slightly at the top of the pushaway and thus enlarging the arc of your pendulum swing, or by increasing your distance from the foul line, thereby

making yourself take larger steps and speed up your delivery.

2. *Make your hook wider* by assuming a sideways position a little to the right of where it would ordinarily be.

3. *Accelerate your ball's english* by moving your index finger closer to your middle finger and your pinky further away from your ring finger.

If your ball continues to hook readily after you have tried all of the above, you might want to experiment with an exaggerated form of the hook ball release (sometimes referred to as *curve ball release*). This release was very popular among bowlers until about twenty years ago, when bowling centers almost exclusively used shellac finishes on their lanes. It results in a counter-clockwise semi-spin like that of the hook ball proper but in a wide left-to-right-to-left arc. It is comparable to the toss of a boomerang. There are a number of ways of executing it, the least difficult and most promising of which is as follows: place your hand in the eleven o'clock position and bring your ball back to the left in the backswing. Then, as you release it and follow through, turn your wrist to the left and swing the rest of your arm to the right. As your ball proceeds down the lane, it will gradually move from somewhere to the left of center to the extreme right and then left again, skidding, then rolling like the straight ball and hook ball proper. As with the latter, the upward action of your hand during the follow-through produces your ball's semi-spin.

While the exaggerated hook or curve ball release may

seem indispensable on a very slow lane, I must warn you that there are a number of serious disadvantages to it. First, because it has to travel a greater distance than either the hook or straight ball, this ball's destination is not as predictable. It has more of an opportunity to get into trouble, no matter how accurate your aim, and it also loses its initial driving force as it makes its arc. Curve balls also tend to leave splits more often than either hook balls or straight balls—and difficult ones at that. Finally, it is less versatile—you can never direct it into the extreme right-hand corner to knock out a die-hard 10-pin.

I mention one final type of release, the *back-up ball release*, only as a warning: do not use it under any circumstances. It results in a hook to the right and a clockwise semi-spin—because of this bowlers sometimes refer to it as the *reverse hook ball release*. It is comparable to a slice in tennis or golf. You execute it (hopefully by mistake) by placing your hand in the three, two, or one o'clock position. The ball skids and rolls like the others two-thirds of the way down the lane, but then it hooks to the right into the pindeck with a clockwise semi-spin. This hook to the right and semi-spin are produced by the upward action of your hand in the three, two, or one o'clock position during the follow-through. The awkward hand position—think about it—makes this type of release almost impossible to control.

Step E: Following Through

As your ball rolls off your fingers and begins making its progress down the lane, your arm should continue its

Path of curve ball.

Path of back-up ball.

Follow-through.

From the Return Rack

smooth forward motion until it is about level with your shoulders. The back of your hand should be parallel with the floor if you are rolling a straight ball and tilting to the right if it is a hook ball, with your thumb down in either case. Your arm should appear to be reaching out for the pins.

Executed correctly, the follow-through is as important to effective bowling as it is to performing well in sports like tennis and basketball. In bowling the follow-through gives your ball direction and causes it to rotate. Failure to follow through properly will result in real headaches. For instance, if you stop your arm short at the moment of release, your ball will be dropped or lofted. If you jerk your arm to the right or left, your ball will also be jerked that way and consequently zoom off course.

Delivering your ball to the foul line in steps co-ordinated with armswings and releasing it there with full confidence that you are controlling it and not it you is largely a matter of practice and patience, and don't let anyone tell you differently. This said, here are some tips to make life easier for you while you are learning or re-learning the basic bowling techniques described in this chapter.

Before attempting the pendulum swing, whether at your bowling center or at home, construct your own pendulum by tying a weight to a piece of string eighteen inches long and observe how it behaves when you swing it back and forth from the height of your shoulder. Note especially that the pendulum does not go as high in its backward swing as in its forward swing. Should you try and force it to go as high in its backward swing, it will move forward in a jerky manner. Now stand before a mirror and, keeping your shoulders facing straight ahead, swing your arm back and forth. Note that, like your pendulum, its forward swing is considerably higher than its backswing. As a matter of fact, its forward swing is shoulder high, while its backswing is only twelve to fifteen inches from your hip. This is the way your arm should swing during the four-step delivery. The secret to preventing your backswing from going beyond manageable heights is to *keep your shoulders facing straight ahead* from the beginning of the pushaway to the very end of the follow-through.

It is a good idea to practice your armswing and four steps separately before co-ordinating them, but while doing one, try to keep the other in mind. If you are practicing these techniques at home, a flat iron makes a good substitute ball. Your four steps should be performed on a smooth surface at least fifteen feet in length marked off at one end by a piece of adhesive tape.

Co-ordinating your armswings with your footsteps may be a little tricky, so perhaps it is best to try the whole thing without a ball first. Concentrate on making your progress to the foul line smooth, continuous, and rhythmic both with and without a ball. Right-out, left-down, right-back, left-forward. Sometimes it helps to think of it as a four-step dance—first, right-out; second, left-down; third, right-back; fourth, left-forward.

When you reach the point of feeling that your co-ordination is perfect or near-perfect, try to arrange with the proprietor of your local bowling establishment for a lane without the pins where you can practice bowl (sometimes called *shadow bowling*). Then, finally, after your body has reacted and adjusted to the all-important additional factors of ball and lane, do it with the pins—but try to keep your attention focused on your form. There will be plenty of time and opportunity later for smashing the pindeck to smithereens.

As for releases, concentrate on the "straightness" of your straight ball and the hooking action and semi-spinning motion of your hook ball. It may be a good idea to practice releases first without the ball, then with the ball but without the pins, and finally with both. If at any time you begin rolling back-up balls, check your hand position; it is probably incorrect. Mentally note each succeeding

BOWLING FOR EVERYONE

change of hand position so that you can make the successful one a constant.

A good general check on your releases can be kept by examining your *ball track*, a band of oil and dust that will build up on the ball's surface during the course of a bowling session. Whatever release you use, your track should be narrow; if it is wide you are doing something inconsistently and should review each of your movements carefully. Also, except in the instance of the straight ball release mentioned below, the track should never pass across the thumbhole. If it does, there is probably something wrong with your follow-through, and this should be corrected, as a ball's progress will be impeded if it rolls over its thumbhole. The track of a properly-released straight ball should bisect your ball by running through the center of the bridge. Note that if a house ball is used, it will also run across the thumbhole; this is the only instance in which the track should go over the thumbhole. The track of a genuine hook ball should run around a third of your ball, that part of it below the thumbhole. If it circumscribes less than a third, your ball is spinning fully. Try to correct this fault, watching for a difference in your ball's rotation. If you have difficulty observing this, stick a small piece of adhesive tape above the bridge or have your pro shop insert a few small white dowels there and keep your eyes on it or them as your ball moves down the lane. Because of its track, this kind of hook ball is generally referred to as a *three-quarter roller*. Also acceptable but not as desirable is a *full roller*, a hook ball whose track bisects the ball by passing over the space between the thumbhole

a. Dust track on straight ball.

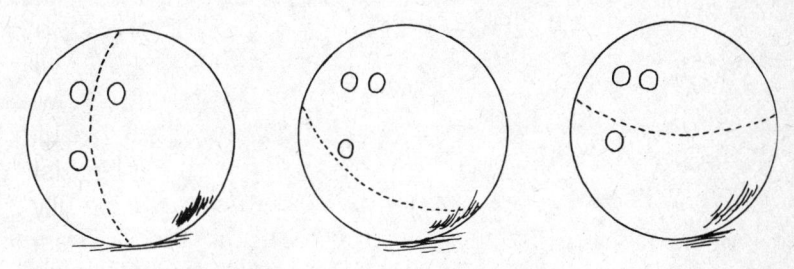

b. Track on three-quarter roller hook ball.

c. Track on full roller hook ball.

and the two fingerholes. This kind of hook ball is achieved by placing the hand in the nine o'clock position, which is not as taxing on the wrist as the eleven or ten o'clock positions, but which gives your ball less semi-spin and therefore is less devastating on the pindeck.

After mastering the hook ball release, practice on different kinds of lanes and teach yourself to vary the release in the ways suggested above according to the lane. At the same time, you might want to try your hand at the more difficult version, the full roller. Note that the track of a full roller should run between the thumb and fingerholes.

Now you are ready to turn your attention to the second moment of truth in bowling: that split second when your ball arrives at the pindeck.

4
STRIKES AND SPARES

Now and then you come across a bowler who speaks of being lucky. He made a certain strike or converted such and such a spare, he will tell you, even though the ball hit a particular pin *lightly* or on the extreme side, *heavily* or on the upper-right side, *head on* or dead center, or *Jersey* or *Brooklyn* or cross-over side. Unquestionably, luck plays a part in bowling just as it does in other sports (a good example would be a shot that completely misses

Strikes and Spares   63

the 1-pin, barely hits the 2- or 3-pin, and still results in a strike). But most experienced bowlers know that luck seldom plays a consistent part in their game. More than likely, if you roll such a strike, someone will remark, and rightly so, "I'll bet you can't do that again!" To play a consistently superior game, you have to develop your bowling skills to the best of your ability. In terms of strikes and spares, this means learning how your hook ball and the pins can behave once the former veers into the pindeck area. You also must know how to use this knowledge to your best advantage.

There are two ways of knocking down a pin: directly, with your ball, or indirectly, with another pin. You can knock down a whole line of pins directly with your ball, or you can have your ball hit directly only the first pin on a line and then let it start a reaction that finishes off the work. It is generally wise to combine the two ways in your strategy, remembering above all this one important fact: a ball veering left into the pindeck that *hits the right side or center of a pin will have its course deflected to the right or straight back*. Take as an example the 6-10 spare. There are two ways of attempting to convert it, but the better is to have your ball hit the right side of the 6-pin. This done, its leftward course will be deflected backward to the right toward the 10-pin, which it should also take out.

You want to knock down as many pins as possible with a given roll of the ball. Let's call the total number of pins you want to take out your *ultimate target*, and the pin nearest you the *key pin*. The latter, when hit, makes things

64 BOWLING FOR EVERYONE

happen on the pindeck, just as the trigger of a gun, when pressed, makes it fire. The key pin can 1) knock down another pin that knocks down another pin, thus setting off a chain reaction along a line of pins, and 2) can, if struck on the right or center, deflect the course of your ball to a pin on its right, which may begin another chain reaction. In the 6-10 spare example, your ultimate target consists of the 6- and 10-pins; the 6-pin is the key pin. Your ball's course will be deflected toward the 10-pin upon impact with the right side of the 6-pin.

Each particular pindeck situation requires its own strategy; this includes what part of the key pin—right or left, sometimes center—your ball should come in contact with. Let's refer to that part of the key pin as your *initial target*. Your initial target for a strike is always the same: the upper-right side of the 1-pin; your ball should then hit only three other pins, the 3-, 5-, and 9-pins. Here is how it works: the ball is deflected from your initial target to the extreme left side of the 3-pin, where it resumes its course to the left, hitting the upper-right side of the 5-pin and being deflected to the right once again, this time taking out the 9-pin. During its progress three chain reactions of diminishing intensity should occur among the remaining pins. The 1-pin should spin backward to the left at the 2-pin; the 2-pin then spins the 4-pin, and the 4-pin to the 7-pin. The 3-pin should spin to the right to the 6-pin and the 6-pin to the 10-pin. The 5-pin should spin to the left to the 8-pin.

For most spares you have a choice of strategies. For instance, there are two possible ways of converting the 6-10 spare. One of these, is to hit the right side of the

Strikes and Spares   65

6-pin, thereby causing your ball's course to be deflected toward the 10-pin. The other is to have the 6-pin take out the 10-pin, and for this to happen your initial target must be the left side of the 6-pin, as hitting it there—and only there—will make it fall toward the 10-pin. But here as in most cases, one way is preferable to the other. The first way, hitting the right side of the 6-pin and having your ball take out the 10-pin, is better strategy than the second, for one very good reason: to cause your ball's course to be deflected toward the 10-pin, you can hit the 6-pin *anywhere on its right side*, but to make the 6-pin fall toward the 10-pin, your ball must come in contact with the 6-pin *at a very particular point on its left side,* to be precise, the upper-left side.

How do you decide which of two ways of handling a spare is better? By considering the alternatives carefully, bearing in mind that your hook ball, with its unique pattern of behavior, is your sole offensive weapon. Your choice should always be the plan that seems to offer you the greatest chance of success with the least amount of risk. In the pages that follow, you will find suggestions to aid you in aiming your ball and in the selection of strategies for individual spares. By all means, do not hesitate to consult them as often as is necessary, even on the lanes if this proves helpful.

Aiming Your Ball

You are on the approach. You've just determined your distance from the foul line. Before beginning your delivery, you must take aim. Aiming the ball consists of four separate actions: determining your sideways position on the approach, aligning your shoulder and arm with some point at the end of the lane, angling your body in relation to your ultimate target, and focusing your eyes somewhere. Once you have determined your aiming, you should maintain it through the delivery to the very end of your follow-through. Let us consider each of these four actions in turn.

1. *Determining your sideways position on the approach*. Most pro's recommend that you relate your sideways position to your ultimate target. For the strike delivery and to convert spares located in the center of the pindeck (for example, the 1-2-5 spare), they tell you to stand in the center of the approach (*strike position*); for spares on the left side of the pindeck (for example, the 2-4-7 spare), somewhere to the right of center; and for those on the right (for example, the 6-10 spare), somewhere to the left. In part I agree with them—strikes should, of course, be attempted from the center of the approach, and right-side spares from the left of center. But as for the rest, my many years of critical observation on the lanes have taught me that most center spares are more successfully handled by the amateur from the right or left of center and some left-side spares, from the left of center. This means that in general I believe in relating your sideways position to your choice of strategy or initial target, rather than to your ultimate target. Since I have in mind specific situations, let's reserve discussion of them for the

Strikes and Spares

next section of this chapter, which deals with individual shots. Suffice to say here that your *exact* position to the left of center for right-side spares and to the right of center for ordinary left-side spares ought to be determined according to the composition of your ultimate target. A good rule of thumb to follow is this: if a right-side spare includes the 10-pin, or an ordinary left-side spare the 7-pin, you ought to stand to the extreme left or right; if neither of them does, then stand closer to the center; stand closest to the center for spares with the 2-, 3-, or 5-pin.

2. *Aligning your shoulder and arm*. In order to allow for the hooking action of your ball, it is generally wise to align your shoulder and arm with an area somewhere to the right of the key pin rather than with the key pin itself. Let's refer to this "area" as your *ostensible target*. How far to the right of the key pin your ostensible target should be depends upon the location of your initial target. Many pro's tell you that if it is the left side of the key pin, your ostensible target is *slightly* to the right; dead center, *farther* to the right; the right side of the key pin, even *farther* to the right. Let me recommend the set of formulas below

Initial Target	Ostensible Target
some part of the 2-, 4-, or 7-pin	8-pin
some part of the 1-, 5-, or 8-pin	9-pin
some part of the 3-, 6-, or 9-pin	10-pin
some part of the 10-pin	where the overhead light falls on the right-hand channel

68   BOWLING FOR EVERYONE

as possibly yielding more effective results; they involve considering spatial relationships rather than focusing around a single pin.

For what might be even greater accuracy and a more startling finish, align your shoulder and arm with the right side of the back pin if your initial target is the left side of the key pin, with the area immediately to the right of the back pin if your initial target is the center of the key pin, and further to the right if your initial target is the right side of the key pin.

3. *Angling your body*. Your body should face your

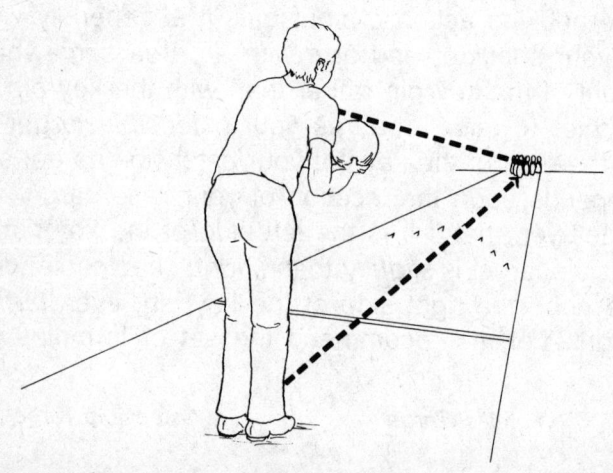

Angling your body for a strike. Note that shoulder and arm are in line with the 3-pin (your ostensible target), and the big toe of your left foot is in line with the 1-pin (key pin in this case).

ultimate target squarely. To take some of the guesswork out of this, let me suggest the following simple maneuver: having assumed your position on the approach and aligned your shoulder and arm with your ostensible target, place the big toe of your left foot in line with the key pin.

4. *Focusing your eyes*. Here there are two generally recognized procedures: keeping your eyes on the key pin (called *pin bowling*) or on some lane markers in line with it (*spot bowling*). There are a whole host of other focusing procedures which combine these two during various phases of your progress to the foul line. In my opinion these procedures are unsatisfactory because they involve removing your attention from the immediate problem of proceeding to the foul line in a straight line. The result is that you tend to *drift* from your sideways position during your delivery, and your ball is released way off course. To avoid this, let the angling of your body—where your shoulder and arm and the big toe of your left foot are pointing—take care of the direction of your ball and keep your eyes fixed on your feet and their destination.

By way of summary, let me explain the difference between how a conventional bowler and I would take aim to convert the 6-10 spare. Since this spare is located on the right side of the pindeck, both the conventional bowler and I would assume a sideways position to the left of center, and since the ultimate target includes the 10-pin, this would be extreme left. Assuming that our strategy is the same and the initial target is the right side of the 6-pin, both of us would align our shoulder and arm with an area

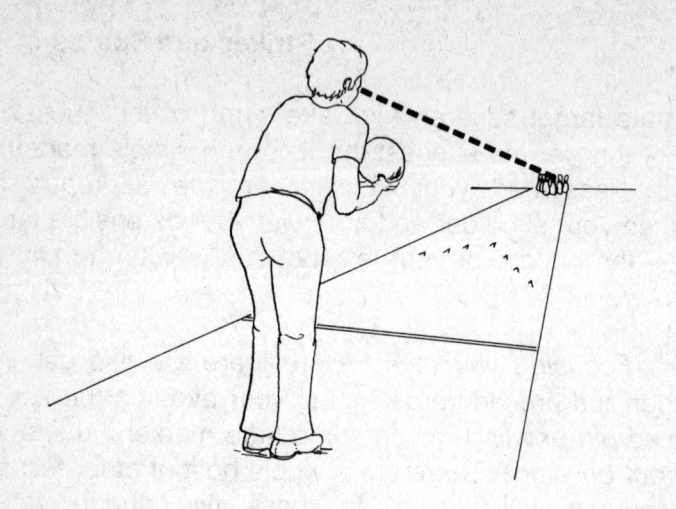

Pin bowling for strike.

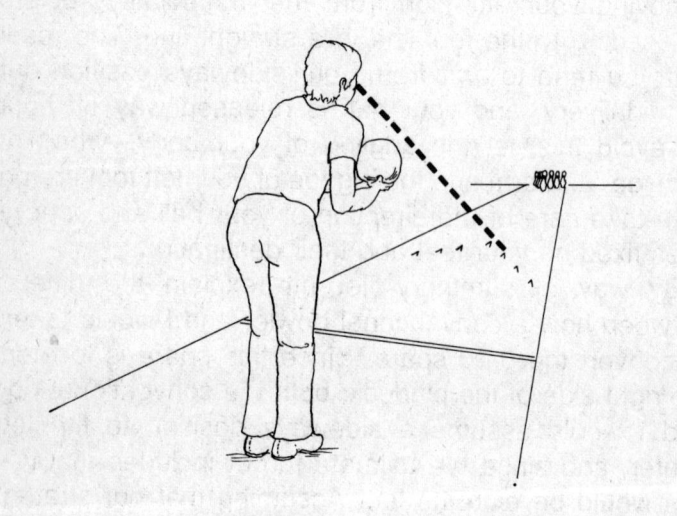

Spot bowling for strike.

far to the right of the 6-pin; for possibly greater accuracy, I might choose instead the area far to the right of the 10-pin. He would turn and face the 6- and 10-pins as it seemed best to him; I would simply move my body slightly so that the big toe of my left foot was in line with the 6-pin. From pushaway to follow-through, he would keep his eyes on the 6-pin or some preselected lane markers leading to it, or possibly shift his eyes from one to the other in some fashion; my eyes would be focused on the floor directly ahead of me. The result would be that during the follow-through his arm might and then again might not be pointing to that area far to the right of the 6-pin; mine definitely would be.

Aiming and Strategy for Individual Shots

So far we've been speaking in generalizations, using a single spare as an illustration. Now it is time to talk about individual shots. Throughout this section we'll be concerned with strategy and sideways position.

The Strike.
As for the strike—the legitimate strike, of course, not the lucky strike—what I have to say is largely a matter of recapitulation. Your strategy is always the same: to hit the upper-right side of the 1-pin, the extreme left side of the 3-pin, the upper-right side of the 5-pin, and the 9-pin, and thereby precipitate chain reactions that will send all of the other pins sprawling—the 1-pin beginning such a reaction

72 BOWLING FOR EVERYONE

along the left edge of the pindeck (2-, 4-, 7-), the 3-pin along the right edge (6-, 10-), and the 5-pin back to the left (8-). Your sideways position is always the same: the center of the approach.

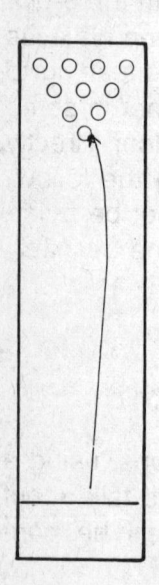

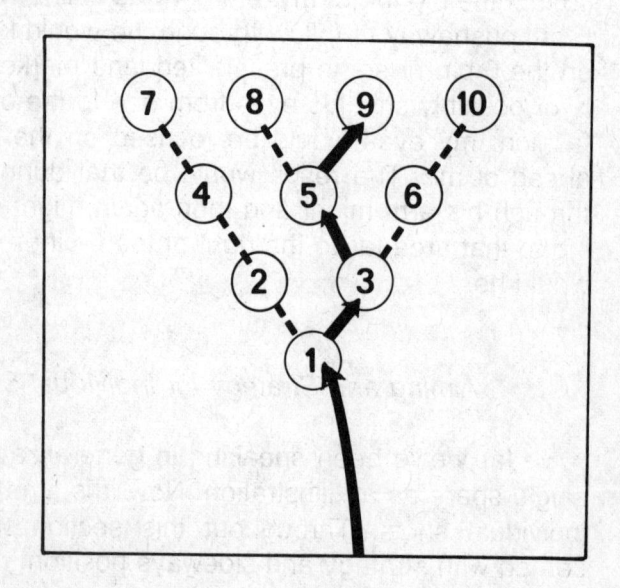

The strike. The diagram shows strategy for the legitimate strike. The heavy solid line represents the bowling ball as it should move within the pindeck area. Dotted lines represent the movement of pins knocking off other pins. The long rectangular box on the left shows the approximate path of the ball (a hook ball in this and all subsequent diagrams). Note the pindeck has been enlarged out of proportion for purposes of illustration.

Strikes and Spares 73

Right-side Spares.
 No matter what the situation, your sideways position for right-side spares is *always* to the left of center. For spares involving any two pins along the right edge of the pindeck (for example, 1-3, 3-6), use the same strategy as for the 6-10 spare, namely consider the right side of the key pin your initial target with the idea of knocking out the pin to its right with your ball. The advantage of this strategy, you will recall, is that you can hit the key pin anywhere on its right side to cause your ball's course to be deflected along the right edge; whereas to make the key pin knock down the other pin, your ball must come in contact with an exact spot on its left side. It is advisable to try more or less the same strategy for the 1-3-6, 3-6-10, and 1-3-6-10 (*right fence*) spares. After your ball's course is deflected to the second pin, either the ball or that pin will take out the third,

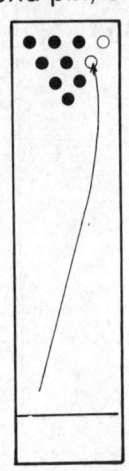

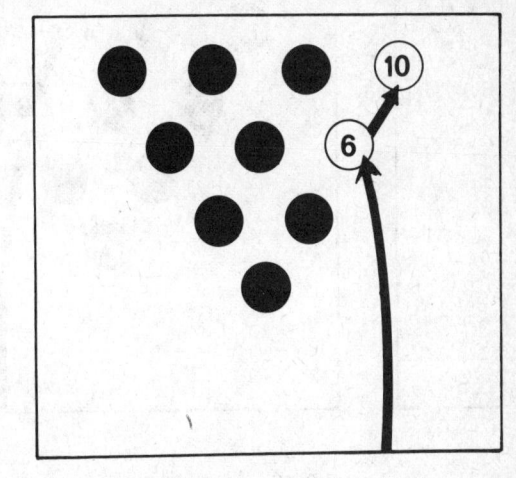

The 6-10 spare.

The 6-9-10 spare.

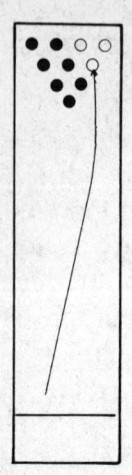

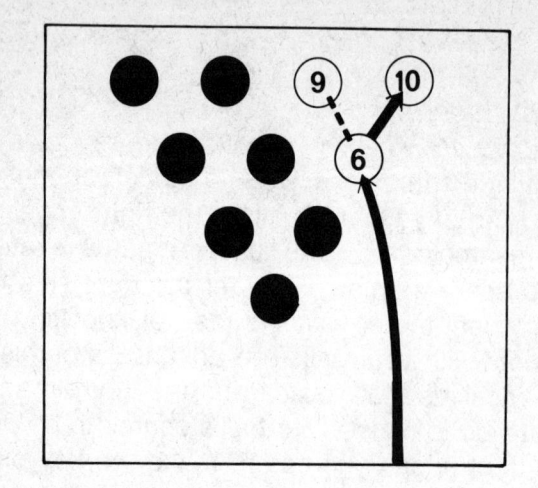

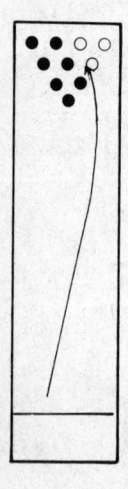

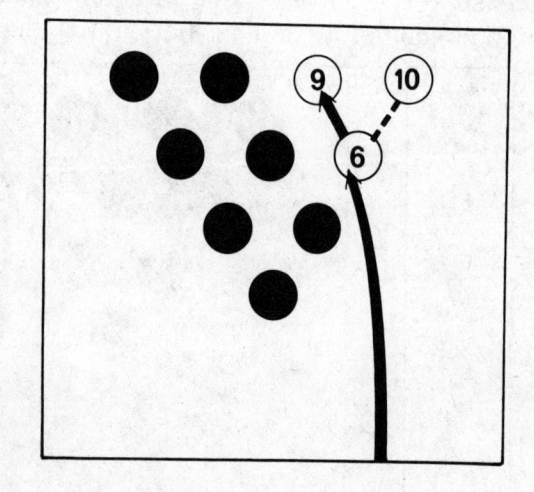

The 6-9-10 spare, alternate strategy.

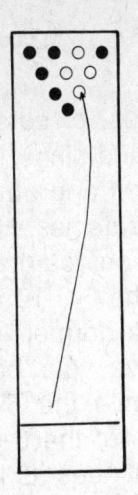

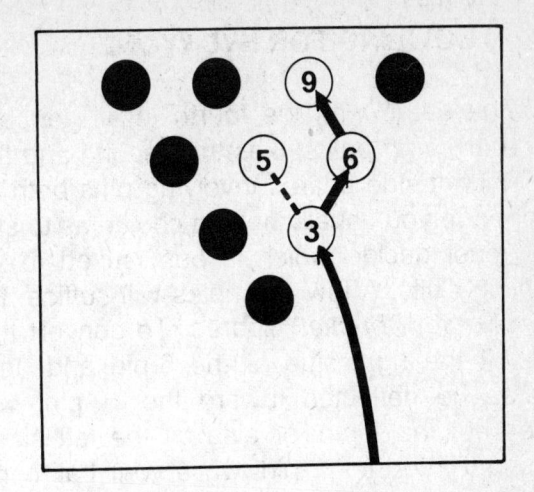

The 3-5-6-9 spare.

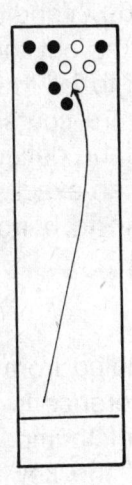

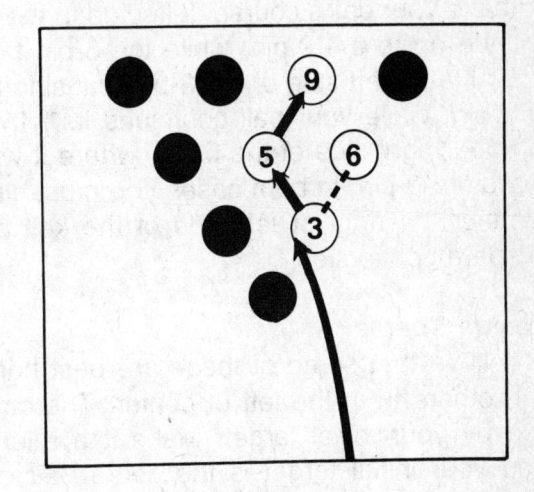

The 3-5-6-9 spare, alternate strategy.

and the same with the fourth; it all depends, of course, on where your ball strikes the second and third pins.

For right-side spares involving pins both on and off the right edge you usually have a choice as to strategies. Here you must decide which is best suited to your particular bowling skills. A few examples will suffice: the 6-9-10 and 3-5-6-9 (*right bucket*) spares. To convert the former, you can hit the right side of the 6-pin and have your ball's course be deflected toward the 10-pin, while the 6-pin takes out the 9-pin; or else hit the left side of the 6-pin, driving it into the 10-pin, while your ball continues its leftward course toward the 9-pin. The choices for handling the 3-5-6-9 are more or less the same but a little more difficult to manage. You can hit the right side of the 3-pin and have your ball's course deflected to the 6-pin and then continue on to the 9-pin, while the 3-pin takes out the 5-pin; or hit the left side of the 3-pin, causing it to fall toward the 6-pin, while your ball continues its leftward course to the upper-right side of the 5-pin, where it will be deflected toward the 9-pin. In both cases you must hit an exact spot on either the right or left side of the key pin to bring off the spare conversion.

Left-side Spares.

I believe that some of these are best handled from the right, others from the left of center. The difference is dictated by your initial target. Make it a rule of thumb that when your initial target is the center left of the key pin, your sideways position is to the right of center; when anywhere else on the key pin (upper left, upper right, dead

Strikes and Spares 77

center), to the left. Choosing the center left of the key pin as your initial target means taking full advantage of the leftward sweep of your ball without any consideration for the possibilities resulting from its course's deflection. This sort of strategy is only used for spares involving pins along the left edge of the pindeck: 1-2, 2-4, 4-7, 1-2-4, 2-4-7, 1-2-4-7 (the *left fence*). Once having hit the key pin on the center left, the ball will proceed along the left edge, knocking down as many pins as are standing there. And, of course, the advantage of this strategy over that of hitting the key pin on the upper-right side, driving it into the next pin and so forth, is that you can accomplish your aim by touching anywhere on the center left—your impact on the upper right must be exact.

For left-side spares with pins both on and off the left edge you usually have a choice of strategies, and again

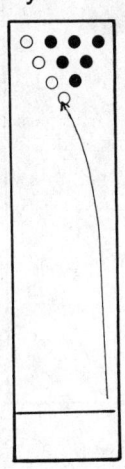

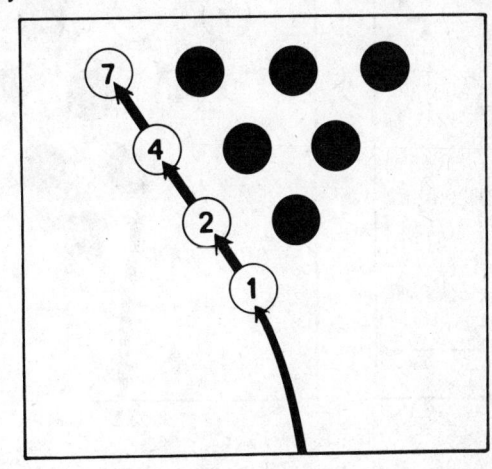

The 1-2-4-7 spare.

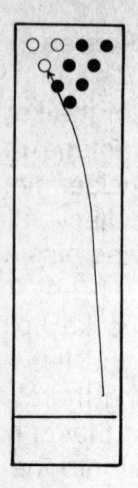

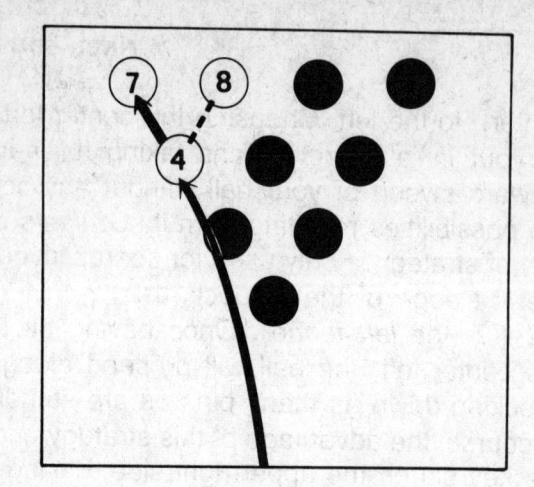

The 4-7-8 spare.

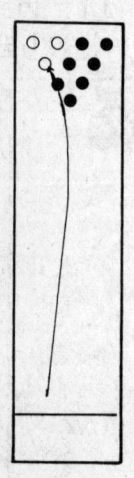

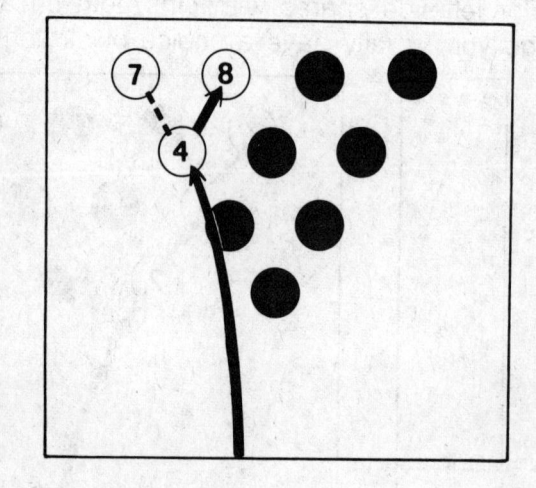

The 4-7-8 spare, alternate strategy.

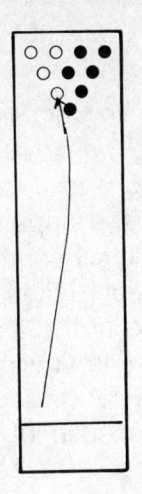

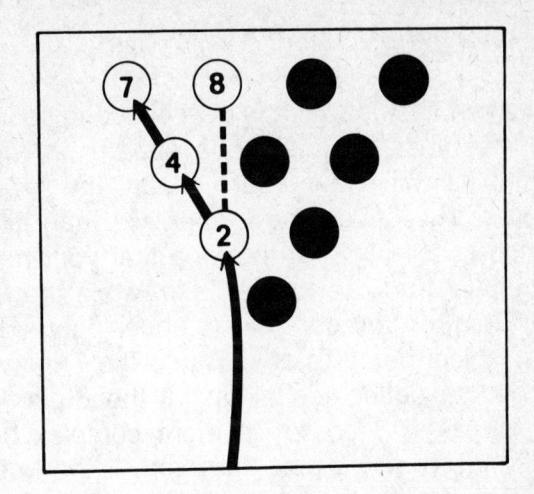

The 2-4-7-8 spare.

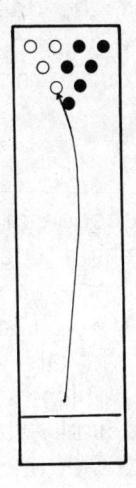

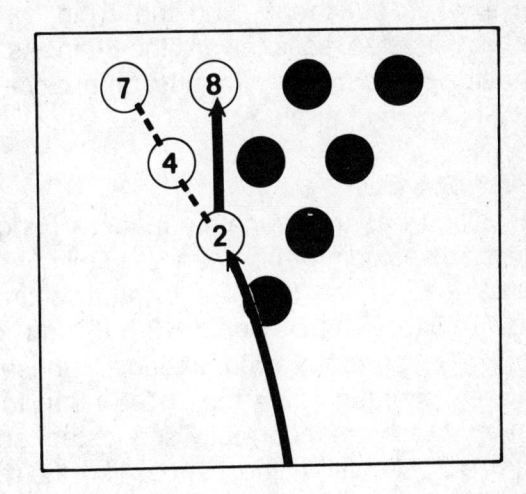

The 2-4-7-8 spare, alternate strategy.

you must decide which is best suited to your bowling skills, as you must for analogous spares on the right. A few examples will show what I mean: the 4-7-8 and 2-4-7-8 spares. To convert the former, you can hit the upper-left side of the 4-pin with the idea that your ball will continue its leftward course to the 7-pin, while the 4-pin takes out the 8-pin; or you can hit the upper-right side of the 4-pin, your object being to drive it into the 7-pin while your ball, its course deflected, takes out the 8-pin. The strategies for the 2-4-7-8 are even more complex because of the presence of the 2-pin. You can hit the upper-left side of the 2-pin so that it falls backward toward the 8-pin while your ball continues its leftward course to the 4- and 7-pins; or else you can hit the upper-right side of the 2-pin so that it takes out the 4- and the 7-pin, while the ball, its course deflected, sails toward the 8-pin. As with analogous right-side spares, your aim must be pretty accurate regardless of choice of strategy.

Center Spares.

Tradition has unfortunately made a hodgepodge of this category, assigning three almost totally unrelated types of spares to it: those that are located in the center of the pindeck, like the 1-3-5 and 1-3-5-8, and for which strike strategy is correctly recommended; those that are also centrally situated, like the 1-2-5, but for which strike strategy has been incorrectly suggested; and finally, those that are not really in the center, like the 1-3-6-9, and for which strike strategy has also been erroneously prescribed.

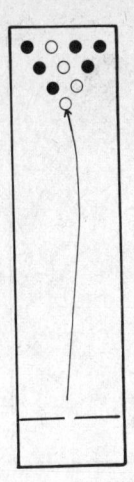

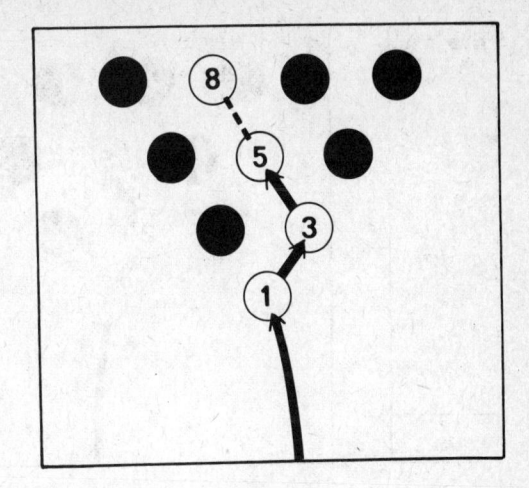

The 1-3-5-8 spare.

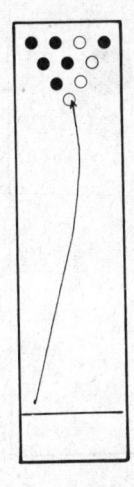

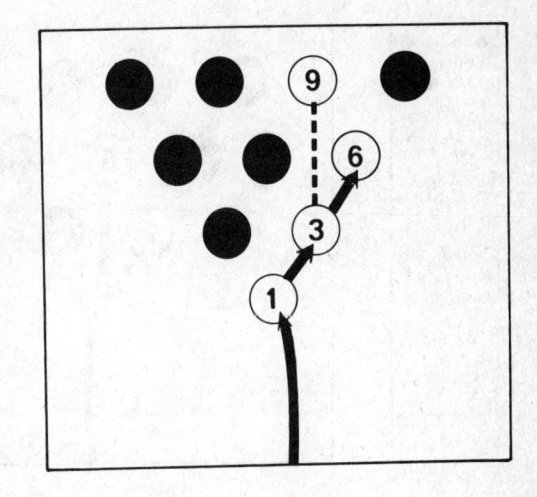

The 1-3-6-9 spare.

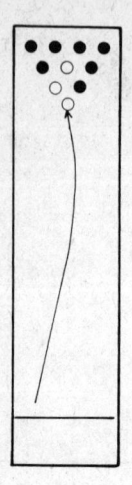

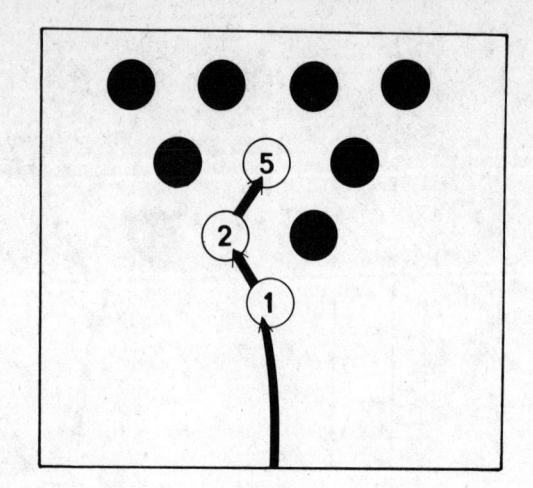

The 1-2-5 spare.

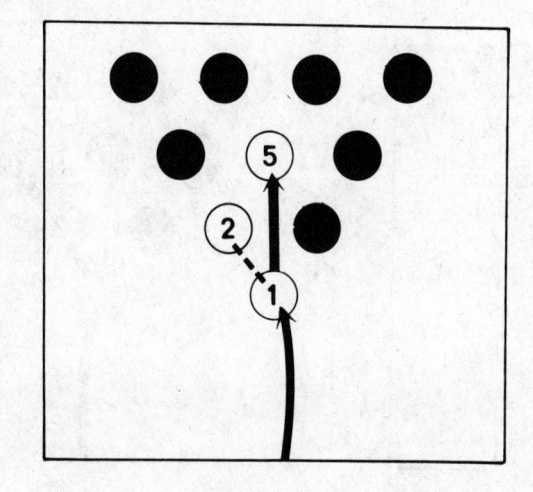

The 1-2-5 spare, alternate strategy.

Strikes and Spares

There are few center spares of the first type. You do use strike strategy for them; this means assuming a sideways position in the center of the approach, and considering as your initial target an exact spot on the upper-right side of the key pin, so that your ball's path begins to follow that of the strike ball (from the 1-pin to the extreme left side of the 3-pin to the upper-right side of the 5-pin). In the case of the 1-3-5-8 spare, the 5-pin will take out the 8-pin, just as it does as a result of a strike ball's action.

As I mentioned above the second and third types of center spares do not take strike strategy; I believe they are more successfully handled by amateurs as right- or left-side spares. Let me suggest how to handle some notorious examples of these kinds of spares, namely the 1-2-5 and 1-3-6-9 spares.

There are two possible ways of converting the 1-2-5, but both involve assuming a sideways position to the left of center. In other words, I suggest you treat it as an "off-edge" left-side spare. You can hit the upper-left side of the 1-pin so that your ball continues its leftward course to the upper-right side of the 2-pin, deflecting the ball to the 5-pin; or hit the upper-right side of the 1-pin, driving it into the 2-pin, while your ball, its course deflected, takes out the 5-pin. As with similar left- and right-side spares, both ways demand the utmost accuracy.

There is only one good way to knock out 1-3-6-9, and that is to treat it as a right-side spare, assuming a sideways position to the left of center. Concentrate on having your ball hit the upper-right side of the 1-pin so that its course is deflected to reach the upper-right side of the 3-pin, where its course will again be deflected, this time toward the 6-pin. Meanwhile, the 3-pin will fall backwards toward the 9-pin. Again, accuracy is essential, but at least you have a chance of conversion this way. A strike ball will do you no good at all, despite what some playing pro's have suggested.

Splits.

There are three categories of splits: those involving pins on the same side of the pindeck, for example, 3-10 and 2-7 (the so-called *baby splits*), and 3-9 and 2-8 (*double wood*); those centrally located or traditionally considered center, such as 1-3-9 and 1-3-10; and those with pins on either side of the pindeck, for example, 2-10, 3-8, and 6-7-10.

Right- and left-side splits are handled exactly like ordinary right- and left-side spares. For the 3-10 you use the same strategy as for the 1-3, 3-6, and 6-10; for the 2-7, the same as for the 1-2, 2-4, and 4-7. For a possibly successful conversion of the 3-9, consider as your initial target the dead center of the 3-pin, the idea being to have it or else your ball, its course deflected, take out the 9-pin. As with ordinary right-side spares, your sideways position for this one should be to the left of center. The same strategy should be used for the 2-8, and since your initial target is dead center on the 2-pin—although this cluster is on the left of the pindeck—your sideways position is to the left of center for it too.

The second category of splits, "traditional center" splits,

Strikes and Spares

ought likewise to be handled like ordinary left- and right-side spares. For instance, to convert the 1-3-9 and 1-3-10 I believe you should use more or less the same strategies as for the 1-3-6-9 and 1-3-6-10 respectively.

The last category of splits vary from spares which are fairly difficult to convert to nearly impossible (for example, the 7-10 spare, *bedposts*). Let's pass over the latter in silence and concentrate on those that are at least within the realm of possibility. The trick is to assume a sideways position diagonally opposite the key pin with the idea of driving it into another pin and possibly picking off yet another with your ball. To consider a few examples, your initial target for the 2-10 should be the left side of the 2-pin, the idea being to send it toward the 10-pin, and so your sideways position would be to the right of center. If you hit the upper-right side of the 3-pin of the 3-8 split, you will cause it to fall toward the 8-pin; your sideways position, then, should be to the left of center. By making the right side of the 6-pin your initial target for the 6-7-10 spare, you drive it toward the 7-pin and at the same time make possible the dispatch of the 10-pin by your ball, its course, naturally, deflected. In this case your sideways position should be to the left of center.

Make a list of shots discussed in this chapter and review the strategies suggested for them. When you begin to feel confident about the logic of strategy-making, make a list of shots not discussed in this chapter and see how you do on your own, choosing those that offer the great-

86   **BOWLING FOR EVERYONE**

est amount of success with the least amount of risk or those best suited to your particular bowling skills.

This accomplished, practice aiming for each of these shots, first on the approach without your ball, and finally in conjunction with your delivery, release, and follow-through. And for better results, by all means try my suggestions: align your shoulder and arm with your ostensible target and the big toe of your left foot with the key pin, keep your eyes on what lies directly ahead of you—and then, at the proper moment, let 'er go!

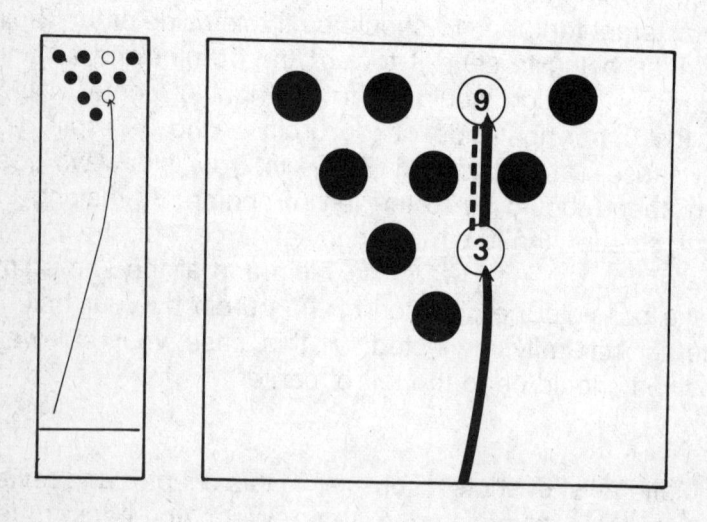

The 3-9 split (double wood).

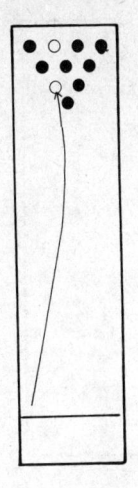

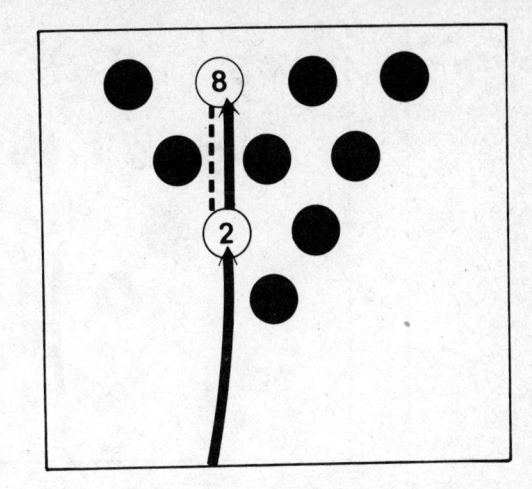

The 2-8 split (double wood).

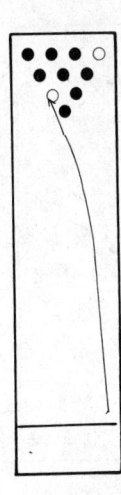

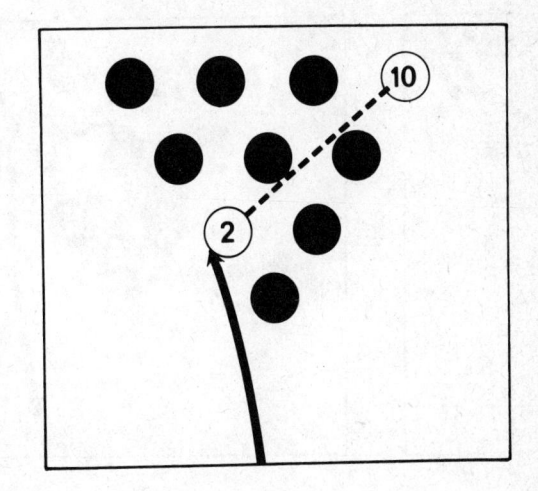

The 2-10 split.

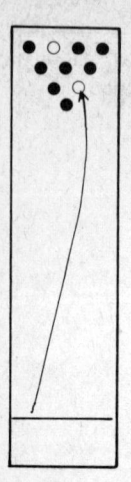

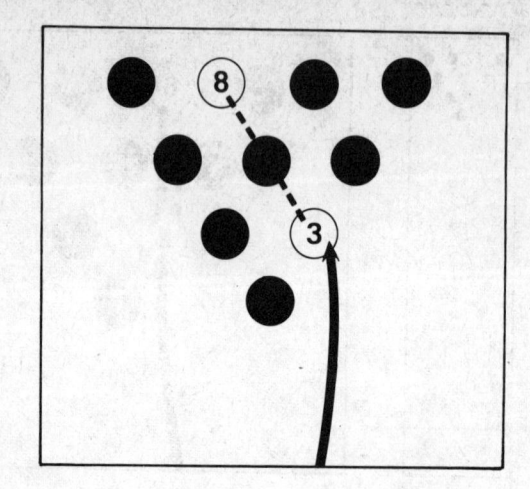

The 3-8 split.

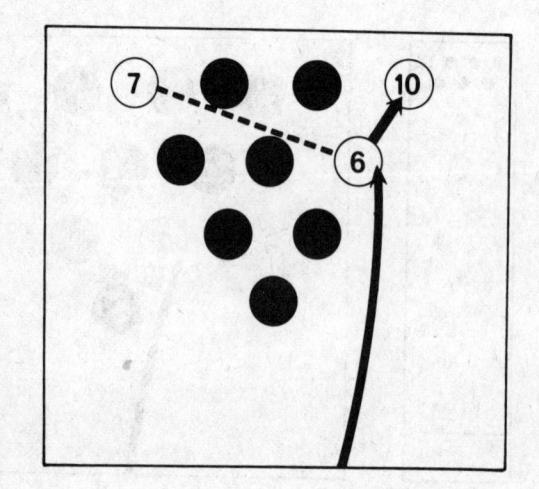

The 6-7-10 split.

5
"PROBLEM" BOWLERS

No one likes to think of himself as a problem, but let's face it—being anything other than a right-handed adult male makes you a bit of a problem in the bowling world, and if you are really set on bowling, you're going to have to make some adjustments. This does not mean that you should ignore everything written in this book so far. On the contrary, you ought to study the rest of the book first,

BOWLING FOR EVERYONE

especially the last two chapters, and then read the particular section of this one that pertains to you.

The Left-handed Bowler

Equipment.

While house balls will do, because their thumbholes are aligned with the center of the bridge, making them interchangeable, you should eventually think about buying your own ball and having the holes drilled to fit your hand. Bear in mind that your thumbhole will be offset to the left of the center of the bridge rather than to the right. The same can be said for shoes. By all means rent them at first, but sooner or later you must have your own. Like the thumbhole of your custom-drilled ball, the soles of your shoes will be the reverse of the usual, the right of leather for sliding, the left of rubber, for braking.

From the return rack to the foul line.

Lifting your ball properly involves placing it in the crook of your right elbow and keeping it there until you are ready to bowl. After determining your position on the approach for a particular shot, assume a stance there by sliding your left foot back so that the tip of your big toe is in line with the center of the instep of your right foot. Bending your knees slightly and tilting your head and trunk forward, shift your ball to your right hand and insert the proper fingers of your left hand into the fingerholes. Then raise and lower your ball until you find a comfortable place for it between your chin and waist.

Left-handed bowler assuming stance.

First step pendulum swing, the pushaway, left-handed.

Second step pendulum swing, left-handed.

94 BOWLING FOR EVERYONE

To execute the pushaway, slide your left foot forward half a step and push your ball out in front of you and slightly to the left. Begin the pendulum swing by moving your right arm to the right for balance, at the same time allowing your left arm with the ball to swing down while you take a normal walking step with your right foot. Then let your left arm swing back and step forward with your left foot. Finally, release the ball while you take a last, somewhat longer, step with your right foot, ending it with a slide, braking yourself with your left foot if necessary. As you are doing this, bend your right leg considerably and tilt your trunk and head forward. Upon reaching the foul line, your body should look like this:

—Your right knee should be bent.
—Your right arm should be out to the right.
—Your head and trunk should be ahead of your right knee.
—Your left arm and leg should be in line with one another.

Follow through by raising your left arm to the level of your shoulders.

While the left-handed straight ball release is effected in the same way as the right-handed one, the hook ball release is quite another matter. On a normal lane, place your hand in the one o'clock position, on a fast lane, in the two or three. You may find the latter necessary because the left sides of lanes—the side you'll be using most—have oilier surfaces due to infrequent use and thus are usually faster than their right sides. As your hook ball proceeds down the lane, again look for a reversal from the norm: it will travel down the left rather than the right side, and it will hook to the right (rather than the left) into the pindeck, half-spinning in a clockwise (rather than counter-clockwise) direction. One of the unique features of left-handed bowling is that your game tends to be more consistent. This is because there are fewer imperfections and less foreign matter on the left sides of lanes—in other words, there are not as many obstacles to interfere with the ordinary progress of your ball.

Strategy and aiming.

Always be aware of the consequences of your ball's rightward hook and half-spinning action; that if you hit the right side of a pin, the ball will continue its rightward movement, but if it's left side or dead center, the ball's course will be deflected leftward or straight back. Consider the 6-9 spare as an example. The preferred strategy for its conversion is to knock out both pins with your ball (rather than sending the 6-pin into the 9-pin). This is accomplished by hitting the left side of the 6-pin, for it will cause your ball's rightward course to be deflected backward to the left toward the 9-pin.

Your sideways position for most right-side spares should be to the left of center, but sometimes to the right. For most left-side spares, just the opposite. As with right-handed bowling, I think that most so-called center spares should be handled as right- or left-side spares—for this, see below concerning individual shots.

Third step pendulum swing, left-handed.

Follow-through, left-handed.

BOWLING FOR EVERYONE

Your ostensible target will be to the left rather than the right of your initial target. If the initial target is the right side of the key pin, your ostensible target is slightly to the left of the key pin; if dead center, farther to the left; and if it's left side, even farther to the left. To determine your ostensible target in relation to the back pins, use the following as a guide:

Initial Target	Ostensible Target
some part of the 2-, 4-, or 8-pin	7-pin
some part of the 1-, 5-, or 9-pin	8-pin
some part of the 3-, 6-, or 10-pin	9-pin
some part of the 7-pin	where the overhead light falls on the left-hand channel

For better results: consider as your ostensible target the left side of the back pin if your initial target is the right side of the key pin; the area immediately to the left of the back pin if your initial target is the center of the key pin; and even farther to the left of the back pin if your initial target is the left side of the key pin.

Upon assuming your position on the approach and aligning your left arm with your ostensible target, angle your body so that it faces your ultimate target squarely by placing the big toe of your right foot in line with the key pin—and, of course, keep your eyes focused on the destination of your feet.

Aiming and strategy for individual shots.

While your sideways position for the legitimate strike is

the same as for right-handed bowlers (the center of the approach) your strategy should be quite different. Your initial target should be the upper-left side of the 1-pin, and your ball should subsequently hit the upper-right side of the 2-pin, the upper-left side of the 5-pin, and the 8-pin. Felling these pins should precipitate chain reactions that will send all of the other pins sprawling, the 1-pin beginning such a reaction along the right edge of the pindeck (3-, 6-, 10-), the 2-pin along the left edge (4-, 7-), and the 5-pin back to the right (9-pin).

A good rule of thumb for right-side spares is that when your initial target is the right side of the key pin, your sideways position is to the left of center, and when the left side or dead center of the key pin, to the right of center. For those involving any pins along the right edge of the pindeck, consider the right side of the key pin your initial

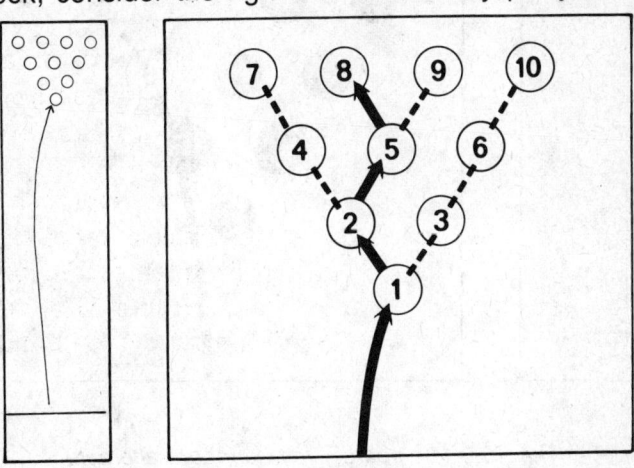

The strike, left-handed.

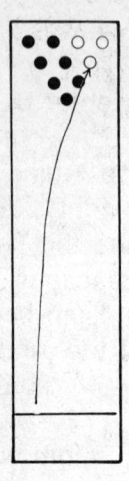

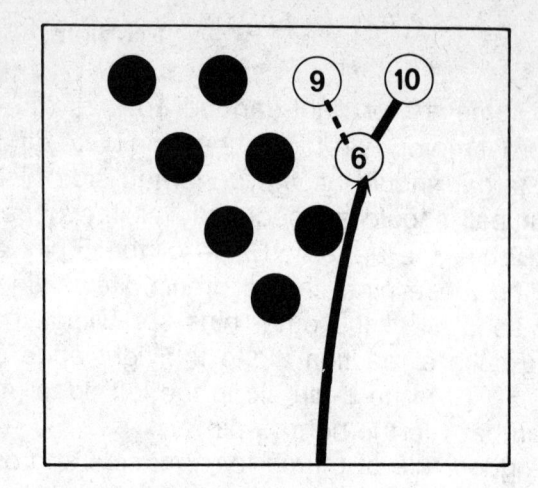

The 6-9-10 spare, left-handed.

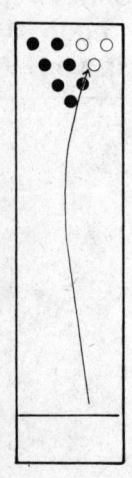

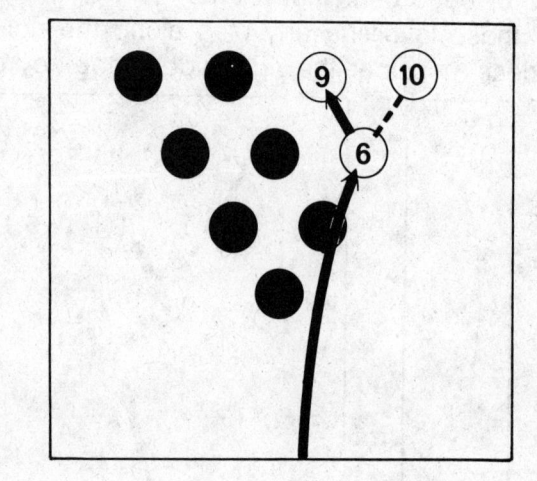

The 6-9-10 spare, left-handed, alternate strategy.

The 2-4-7-8 spare, left-handed.

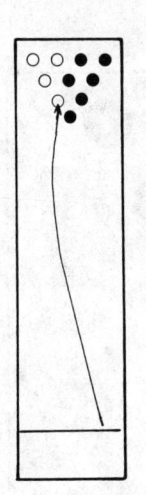

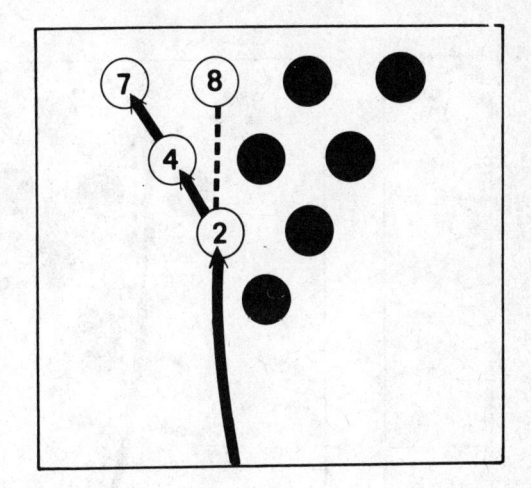

The 2-4-7-8 spare, left-handed, alternate strategy.

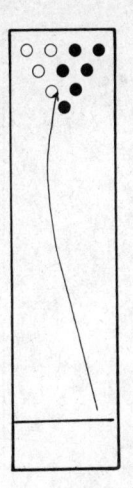

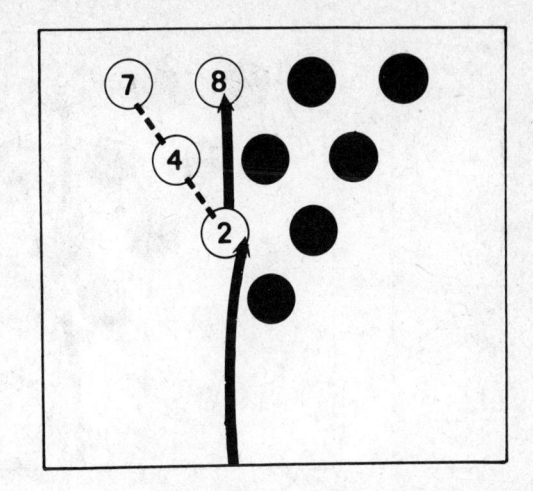

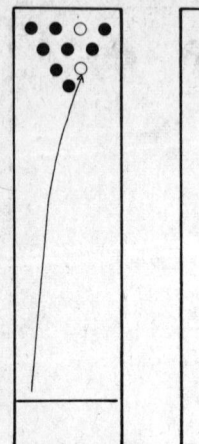

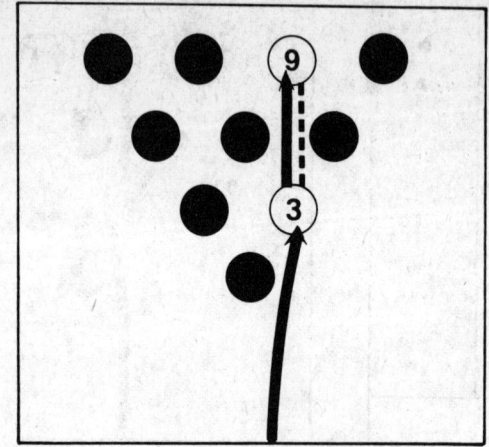

The 3-9 split (double wood), left-handed.

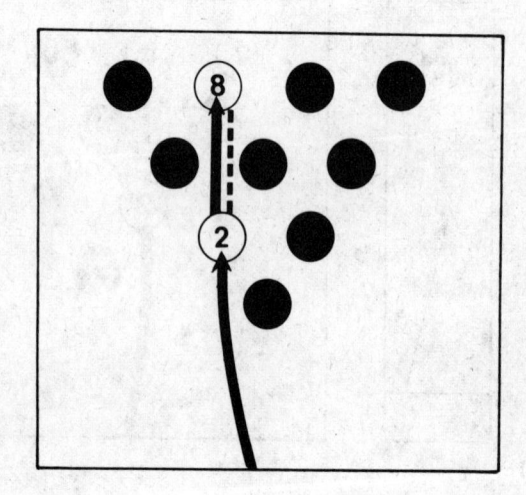

The 2-8 split (double wood), left-handed.

target with the idea of taking advantage of your ball's rightward sweep. For those involving pins both on and off the right edge, you have a choice of strategies, and you must decide which is best suited to your bowling skills. Let the 6-9-10 spare serve as an example. To convert it, you can hit the upper-left side of the 6-pin, sending it into the 10-pin, while your ball, its course deflected, takes out the 9-pin; or else you can hit the upper-right side of the 6-pin, sending it into the 9-pin, while your ball continues its rightward sweep to the 10-pin.

A good strategy to follow for left-side spares is to stand to the right of center when your initial target is the left side of the key pin and to the left when your target is the right side. For those involving any two pins along the left edge, consider the left side of the key pin your initial target with the idea of taking out the pin to its left with your ball, its course deflected there. For spares with more than two pins along the same edge, use more or less the same strategy, assuming that either your ball or the second pin will take out the third and fourth pin, depending, of course, upon where your ball strikes the second and third pins. To convert spares with pins both on and off the edge, you have a choice of strategies, and again you must decide what is best suited to your talents. For example, to dispatch the 2-4-7-8 spare you can hit the upper-left side of the 2-pin, driving it into the 8-pin, while the ball, its course deflected, takes out the 4- and 7-pins; or you can hit the upper right side of the 2-pin, driving it into the 4- and the 4- into the 7-pin, while your ball continues its sweep to the 8-pin.

I have already discussed center spares. Let me simply add that, as with right-handed bowling, strike strategy should only be used for those spares which require it—for example, the 1-2-5 spare.

Splits involving pins on the same side of the pindeck are ordinarily handled like right- and left-side spares. Strategy for the double wood spares, as well as those with pins on both sides of the pindeck, is the same as for right-handed bowling, except that your sideways position for the 3-9 is to the left of center and for the 2-8 to the right.

The Woman Bowler

Leagues.

Most bowling centers have leagues for women and also co-ed leagues. These leagues, plus women's tournaments, come under the jurisdiction of the women's equivalent of the ABC, the Women's International Bowling Congress (*WIBC*).

Equipment.

Unless unusually strong, you will not be able to use as heavy a ball as a male bowler. So if you are a novice, consider beginning with an even lighter ball than your male counterpart, say one weighing between ten and twelve pounds. Gradually progress to a heavier ball, say a thirteen- to a fifteen-pounder.

Your clothes should not be too tight. Make sure that the lower part, whether it be slacks, culottes, shorts, or a plain

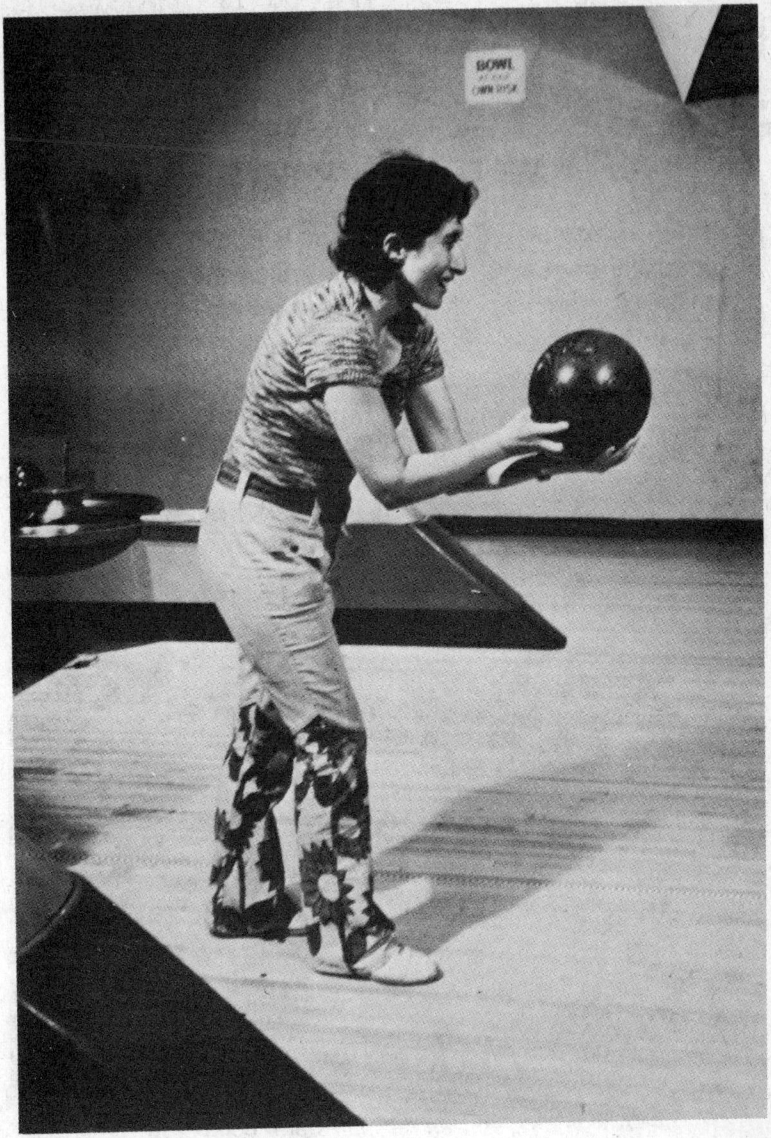
BOWL

106 BOWLING FOR EVERYONE

old skirt, is elasticized at the waist. I prefer to see a woman wearing a semi-full skirt while bowling. In addition to providing maximum comfort, it is graceful and attractive.

From the return rack to the foul line, etc.

Generally speaking, you should follow the same procedures as a man, but since a woman is usually not as strong, you must develop consistent delivery and accurate aim and learn to be content with these as reasonable substitutes for power. I would recommend only one variation, and this concerns the straight ball release. Because a

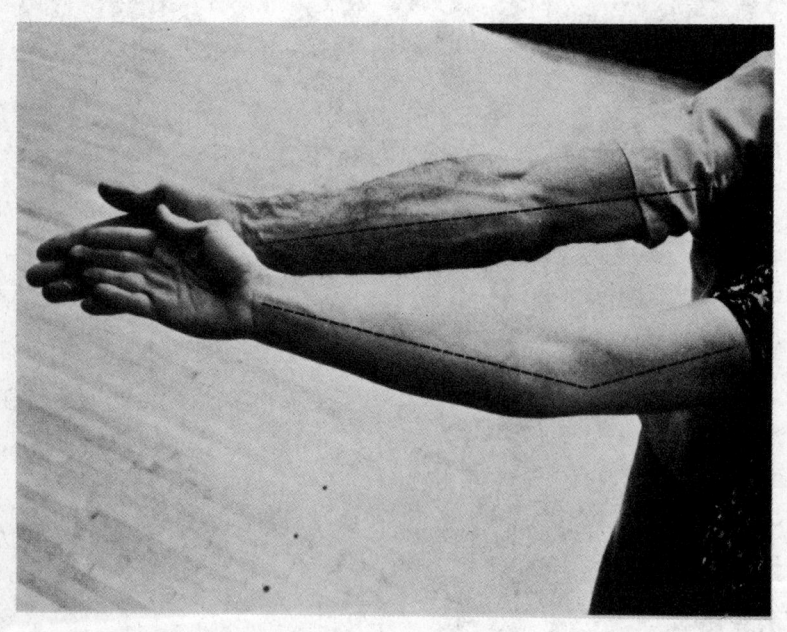

A woman's arm and a man's arm compared.

woman's upper arms meet her forearms at a sharper angle than a man's, your wrist will probably become twisted during this release so that your hand is in the one, two, or three o'clock position when your ball leaves it, resulting in a back-up ball, replete with a clockwise semi-spin. To prevent this, place your hand in the same position you would use for the hook-ball release (at eleven o'clock). Move it slowly upward during the follow-through and you will produce the desired straight flat roll. And, of course, if you want the ball to hook, all you need do is accelerate this upward action.

Junior Bowlers

Leagues.
There are leagues and tournaments for youngsters as well as for women. All of these come under the jurisdiction of the American Junior Bowling Congress (*AJBC*).

Equipment.
The weight of a ball may prove to be a problem if you are small or underweight. So try the adult-sized balls first, but by all means, if you can't manage them, settle for a ten- or eleven-pounder until you get a little bigger.

From the return rack to the foul line, etc.
As with women bowlers, there are no special rules. That is why bowling is called a "family" game.

A junior bowler.

Bowling from the foul line: old person technique.

BOWLING FOR EVERYONE

The Very Young and The Very Old Bowler

Leagues.
Ordinarily you should not begin bowling until you are nine years old, but once started you should never have to quit. Nowadays, with the growing number of active senior citizens, more and more bowling centers have leagues for the elderly, and the ABC sponsors senior tournaments.

Equipment.
The lighter balls, nine to twelve pounds, are practically a must for the very young or very old.

From the return rack to the foul line, etc.
If you have difficulty picking up momentum during your delivery, try a higher pushaway. This will result in a higher backswing and more *oomph*. If the co-ordination of armswings with footsteps proves to be too much like work, forget it and settle for rolling your ball from the foul line. Of course, even this may prove too taxing—but don't give up. Hold your ball with both hands and roll it from between your legs—and don't be self-conscious about it either. You'll never make the 200-or-over class, but you can achieve a fair degree of success this way in your own peer group.

"Problem" Bowlers

The Disabled Bowler

Leagues.
The Bowler's Victory League has divisions for veterans confined to wheelchairs and for the blind. Some bowling centers have special facilities, like a guide rail and sighted scorer for blind bowlers.

Equipment.
Unless your arm is particularly strong, an extra light ball is recommended, at least initially. Don't be disappointed if you have to stick with it. You'd be surprised what you can accomplish with it and a little patience.

From the return rack to the foul line, etc.
Naturally, you will have to make some adjustments, depending upon your disability. If you normally use crutches, you can support yourself on one of them at the foul line and roll the ball from there. The same can be done if you are in a wheelchair, provided that you place the wheelchair at a slight angle to the foul line so that the wheel that protrudes will not get in the way of your arm.

6
BOWLING ETIQUETTE

Besides being well-mannered and a good sport, every bowler ought to be familiar with and conform to what is considered proper behavior on the lanes. Here are some of the most common rules of bowling etiquette:

    1. If it is your turn to bowl, proceed to the approach without delay; if not, remain on your bench.

Bowling Etiquette

2. Never use someone else's ball without his express permission.

3. Don't take any practice slides or swings with your ball unless you are on the approach.

4. If you and the person to your right are both ready at the same time, allow him to bowl first.

5. Never send two balls down a lane in quick succession (called *double-balling*).

6. Between deliveries in a given frame get out of the line of vision of nearby bowlers by leaving the approach until your ball returns.

7. After your second roll leave the approach promptly to make way for the next one up.

8. Wait until a frame is complete to check your score.

7
BOWLING FAULTS AND HOW TO CORRECT THEM

After studying the contents of this book and practicing to the best of your ability, you may nevertheless develop some faults of such a trying nature that they seriously cramp your style. Should this happen, kindly do both of us a favor. Go back and read the book again, perhaps once more after that, paying extra special attention to those passages relevant to your problem. Then, if you still find yourself in the same bind, return to this spot and see

Bowling Faults

if what follows is of any help—some common faults that bowlers are plagued with and suggestions, both common and uncommon, as to their correction.

1. *You do not face your ultimate target squarely.* If a strike is what you are after, make doubly certain that your shoulders are parallel to the foul line; if a spare, to your ultimate target.

2. *The first step of your delivery is out of line.* Try a shorter step or, instead of an actual step, a shuffle.

3. *You pull your shoulder back.* Try a lower pushaway or else consider using a lighter ball.

4. *You swing your arm away from your body.* Practice your pendulum swing with a towel under your upper arm.

5. *Your backswing is too high or not high enough.* Swing a homemade pendulum in front of a mirror and then imitate its movement with your arm.

6. *Your finish at the foul line is awkward or jerky.* Check your ball, shoes, and clothing for an improper fit.

7. *Your release is premature or retarded.* Try tightening or relaxing your thumb grip somewhat. If this does not do the trick, practice releasing your ball four to six inches beyond the foul line, using a folded towel as a marker.

8. *You loft your ball.* Bend your left knee more as you release your ball; this will bring it closer to the floor.

9. *You drift during your delivery.* Practice your four steps on a taped or chalked line, keeping your eyes firmly fixed on it.

10. *Your ball rolls into the channel.* Try giving more momentum to your ball during the follow-through.

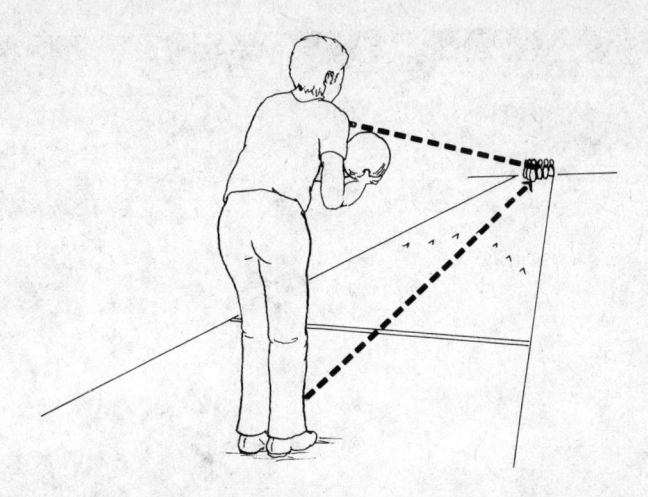

Fault 1: Not facing ultimate target squarely. For a strike your left foot should be aligned with the 1-pin, your right shoulder with the 3-pin. The correct alignment is shown above. Below, right shoulder and left foot are incorrectly aligned with pins too far to the right.

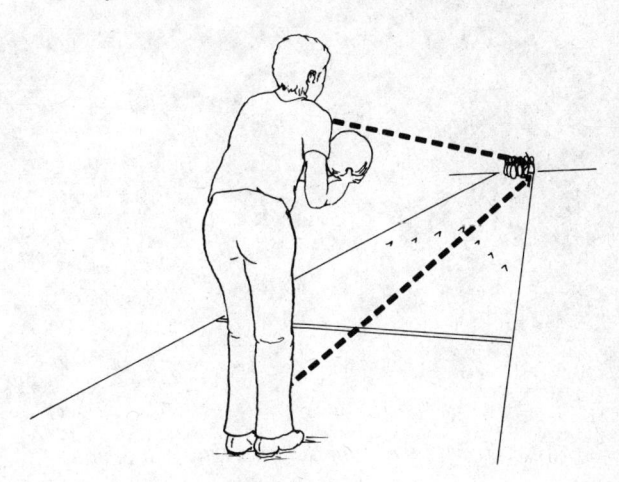

Fault 2: First step pendulum swing out of line.

Fault 3: Shoulder pulling back.

Fault 4: Arm swung from body.

Fault 5: Backswing too high.

Fault 6: Awkward finish at foul line.

Fault 7: Premature release.

Fault 7: Late release.

Fault 8: Loft ball.

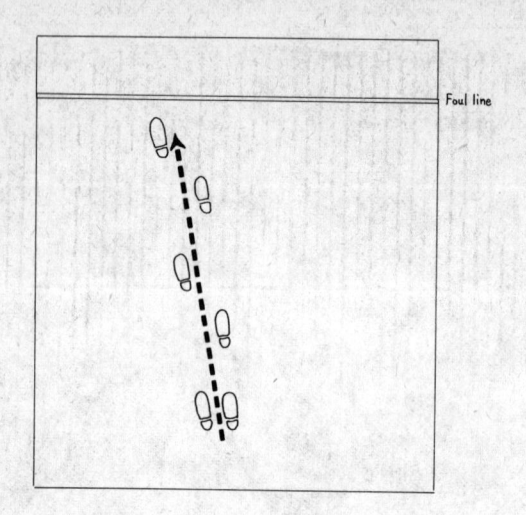

Fault 9: Drifting feet during delivery.

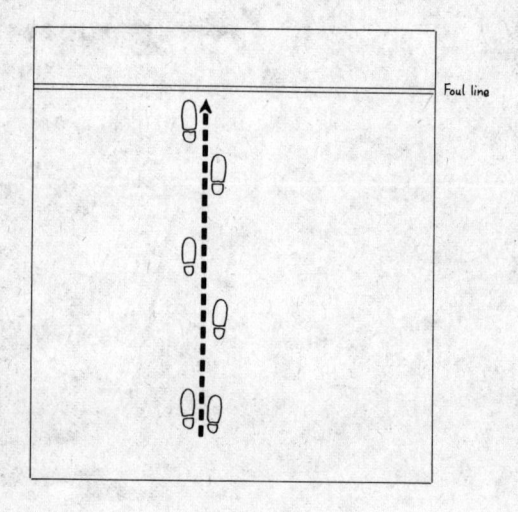

Correct approach.

Fault 10: Channel ball.

GLOSSARY

In addition to those found on the pages of this book, here are some terms commonly used in bowling centers today.

    Apple   The ball.

    Baby split   The 3-10 and 2-7 splits.
    Barmaid   Same as sleeper.

Glossary

Bat out   Same as strike out.
Bed posts   The 7-10 split.
Big ball   An effective hook.
Big ears   The 4-6-7-10 split.
Big fill   Anything over eight on a spare.
Big five   Three pins on one side and two on the other, as the 4-7 on left and 6-9-10 on right.
Big four   The 4-6-7-10 split.
Bolsa   A light or thin hit.
Box   Synonym for frame.
Break   Failure to make a strike or spare in frame.
Broom ball   Same as sweeper.

CC   A 200 game.
Cheese cakes   Lanes on which strikes are easy to get.
Cherry   A ball that chops off the front pin of a spare and leaves standing the pin behind and/or to right or left.
Christmas tree   The 3-7-10 for right-hander; the 2-7-10 for left-hander.
Cincinnati   The 8-10 split.
Clean game   Complete game with no open frames.
Clothesline   Same as left- and right-hand picket fence.
Creeper   Same as powder puff.
Cross alley   To aim to the left from extreme right-hand corner of approach, or to the right from extreme left-hand corner.
Crow hopper   A clawlike, loose grip on ball.

BOWLING FOR EVERYONE

Cutter   A sharp-breaking hook that cuts down the pins.

Dead apple or ball   Ball which fades when it hits pins; ineffective ball.
Deadwood   Pins that have been knocked over by the ball and are lying on the alley or in pit.
Dime store   The 5-10 split.
Dive   A lane on which a ball takes a last-minute big hook or dive to the left.
Dog-leg   The 1-2-10 leave.
Double   Two strikes in succession.
Double pinochle   The 4-6-7-10 split.
Double pinochle with the Ace of Spades   The 4-6-7-10 split plus the 9-pin.
Double wood   One pin directly behind another; the 2-8 and the 3-9 leaves.
Dutch 200   A 200 game made by alternate strikes and spares.
Dutchman   Same as Dutch 200.

Eight-Ten   The 8-10 split.

Faith, hope and charity   Same as Christmas tree.
Fence posts   Same as bed posts.
Field goal   Sending ball between the pins of a split and hitting neither of them.
Fill   The number of pins knocked down following a spare.

Glossary

Fill a frame   To get a strike or spare in a given frame.
Fit-in shot   Any spare requiring exact placement of the ball between two pins to make the shot.
Flat apple or ball   Same as dead apple or ball.
Floater   A ball that goes where the lane lets it go.
Foundation   A strike in the ninth frame.
Four-six   The 4-6 split.
Four-timer   Four strikes in a row.

Getting the count   Same as steal.
Getting the wood   Knocking down a good score.
Go to the route   Same as strike out.
Goal posts   Same as bed posts.
Golden gate   The 4-6-7-10 or big four split.
Grab   Same as dive.
Grasshopper   A good working ball which splashes the pins.
Graveyards   The toughest pair of alleys in a bowling center.
Groove   An apparent depression that carries the ball into the pocket.

Half strike   A setup in which the 2-, 4-, 5-, 7-, and 9-pins are left standing.
Hard way   Same as Dutch 200.
Headpin   The 1-pin.
High board   The condition existing when a board contracts or expands a trifle due to atmospheric conditions, changing course of ball.

BOWLING FOR EVERYONE

High 10 and 30   Western term for high game and high three-game total.
Hold   The fastness of a lane.
Holding lane   Fast lane.
Home lane   Lanes on which bowlers get more strikes than on others; also home lane of a traveling team.
Honey   A good ball.
Hook lane   Slow lane.

In the dark   Same as sleeper.
In there   Ball was a good pocket hit.
Inning   Each bowler's turn.

Jack Manders   The ball goes through middle of 7-10 split.

Kegeler-Kegeler   Synonym for bowler, from German *kegel* (Indian club).
Kick off   Effective delivery of a good ball.
Kindling wood   Light pins.
Kresge   The 5-7 split.

Late ten   A strike in which 10-pin is the last to be knocked down.
Left-hand bucket ⎫
Left-hand dinner bucket ⎬ The 2-4-5-8 leave.
Left-hand dinner pail ⎭
Left-hand picket fence   The 1-2-4-7 leave.
Lily   The impossible 5-7-10 split.

Glossary

Loaf   To put improper hook action on the ball so it fails to come up to objective.

Looper   Hook ball which describes a wide arc; an "out and in" ball.

Louie   In some localities, synonym for headpin.

Make it fit   Trying to make the 4-5, 9-10 or similar splits where both sides of ball must contact pins.

Maples   The pins.

Mark   A strike or spare.

Mother-in-law   The 7-pin.

Mule ears   Same as bed posts.

Murphy   Same as baby split.

Nose hit   To hit a pin dead center.

Out and in ball   Same as curve ball.

Packing   Same as count.

Part of the building   Expression used when 7- or 10-pin stands on a good hit.

Pick   To knock down some pins while leaving others when shooting a spare.

Pinching the ball   Gripping ball too hard and causing an unnatural delivery.

Poison ivy   The 3-6-10 leave.

Powder puff   A slow ball that fails to carry.

Powerhouse   A strike ball that carries all ten pins into the pit.

Puddle   A gutter ball.

Puff ball　　　Same as powder puff.
Pumpkin　　　Same as dead apple.

Rail or railroad　　　Synonym for split.
Rake　　　Same as cutter.
Right-hand bucket　　　⎫
Right-hand dinner bucket　　⎬　The 3-5-6-9 leave.
Right-hand dinner pail　　　⎭
Right-hand picket fence　　　The 1-3-6-10 leave.
Running lane　　　Slow lane.
Runway　　　Approach.

Sandwich game　　　Same as Dutch 200.
Schleifer　　Thin hit strike, similar to spiller type where pins seem to fall one by one.
Shake　　　The 4-6 leave.
Short pin　　A pin, rolling on lane, that fails to hit a standing pin.
Sleeper　　　Hidden or obscured pin.
Slot lane　　　Same as cheese cakes.
Small ball　　A ball that has to hit pins almost perfectly for strikes.
Snake eyes　　　Same as bed posts.
Snow plow　　　Same as cutter.
Soft lanes　　　Same as cheese cakes.
Sour apple　　　Same as dead apple.
Sour apple leave　　　The 5-7-10 leave.
Spiller　　Strike from a thin hit where pins seem to melt away.

Glossary

Splash Strike where pins are knocked off almost instantaneously.
Splash spiller A strike made by a thin hit.
Squeezing Same as pinching the ball.
Steal To get more pins than deserved on a hit.
Stiff lane Fast lane.
Strike out Rolling three consecutive strikes in the tenth frame.
Sweeper Same as cutter.

Tandem Same as double wood.
Tap. Pin left standing on an apparently perfect hit, either the 7-, 8-, or the 10-pin.
Telephone poles Same as bed posts.
Thin hit When the ball hits the headpin lightly.
Throw rocks To throw a lot of good strike balls.
Turkey Three strikes in a row.
Turkey out Same as strike out.

Umbrella ball A heavy or nose hit that results in a strike.

Washout The 1-2-10 or the 1-2-4-10 spare.
Winding them in Making strikes consistently.
Wooden bottles Pins.
Woolworth Same as dime store.
Working ball Ball that moves with good rolling action and produces lots of lively action among pins.

APPENDIX: ABC GENERAL PLAYING RULES

Scoring the Game

Rule 1. a. A game of American Tenpins shall consist of ten frames. Each player shall bowl two balls in each of the first nine frames except when he shall make a strike. A player who scores a strike or spare in the tenth frame shall deliver three balls.

b. A ball is legally delivered when it leaves the bowler's possession and crosses the foul line into playing territory. A bowling ball must be delivered entirely by manual means and shall not incorporate any device either in the ball or affixed to it which is either detached at time of delivery or is a moving part in the ball during delivery except that any person who has had his hand or major portion thereof amputated may use special equipment to aid in grasping and delivering the ball providing the special equipment is in lieu of the amputee's hand.

c. Where an artificial or medical aid is necessary for grasping and delivering the ball because of any other disability of the hand or arm, permission to use the aid in sanctioned competition may be granted by the ABC Executive Secretary's office under the following conditions:

> (1) The aid does not incorporate a mechanical device with moving parts which would impart a force or impetus to the ball.
> (2) A description or drawing and model of the aid is furnished ABC.
> (3) A doctor's certificate describing the disability together with his recommendation that the aid should be used is furnished ABC.

If permission is not granted, the claimant shall have the right of appeal to the ABC Legal Committee.

Should permission be granted for the use of an artificial or medical aid, a special identification card (not an ABC membership card) will be issued the applicant indicating that the aid may be used in sanctioned competition providing the bowler has a current membership card and the use of the aid is specially authorized by the league or tournament management.

Permission to use the device may be withdrawn for cause.

Strike
Rule 2. A strike is recorded when the player completes a legal delivery and bowls down the full setup of ten pins on the first ball. It is designated by an (x) in the small square in the upper right-hand corner of the frame in which the complete set of ten pins is bowled down with the first ball. The count in each frame where a strike is bowled shall be left open until the player has completed two more deliveries. The maximum count on one strike when followed by a spare is 20.

138 BOWLING FOR EVERYONE

Double

Rule 3. When a player bowls two strikes in succession legally delivered, he shall have scored a double. The count in the frame where the first strike was bowled shall be left open until the player has completed his next delivery. When all pins are down twice in succession the count for the first strike is 20 plus the number of pins knocked down with the first ball of the third frame following. The maximum count on a double figuring a nine pin count on the first ball following the second strike is 29.

Triple or Turkey

Rule 4. In scoring three successive strikes, the player shall be credited with 30 pins in the frame in which the first strike was bowled. Thus, in a game of ten full frames, a player must bowl 12 strikes in succession in order to bowl a game of 300.

Spare

Rule 5. Any player who bowls down the remaining pins with a legally delivered second ball in any frame has scored a spare. A spare is designated by a (/) in the small square in the upper right-hand corner of the frame in which it is made. The number of pins knocked down after the first delivery before the player bowls for the spare should be marked by a small figure in the upper right corner of the frame. The count in such frame proper is left open until the player shall have bowled his first ball in the next frame following, when the number of pins knocked down by the first ball shall be added to the ten pins represented by his spare, and the total shall be credited therein. When a spare is scored in the tenth frame, a third ball shall be bowled in that frame.

Error

Rule 6. A player shall have made an error when he fails to bowl down all ten pins after having completed two deliveries in a given frame provided the pins left standing after the first ball is bowled do not constitute a split. An error is designated by a (—) in the small square in the upper right-hand corner of the frame in which the error is made. The number of pins knocked down after the first delivery, before the player bowls the remaining pins, should be marked in the upper right corner of the frame. The count in every frame where an error is committed shall be recorded immediately following the player's second delivery.

Split
Rule 7. A split shall be a setup of pins remaining standing after the first ball has been legally delivered provided the headpin is down, and

> 1. At least one pin is down between two or more pins which remain standing, as for example: 7-9, or 3-10.
> 2. At least one pin is down immediately ahead of two or more pins which remain standing, as for example: 5-6.

A split is designated by a (0) in the small square in the upper right-hand corner of the frame in which the split occurs. The number of pins knocked down on the first delivery should be marked in the upper right-hand corner before the second ball is rolled.

Pinfall—Legal
Rule 8. Every ball delivered by the player shall count, unless declared a dead ball. Pins must then be respotted after the cause for declaring such dead ball has been removed.

1. Pins which are knocked down by another pin or pins rebounding in play from the side partition, rear cushion, or sweep bar when it is at rest on the pindeck prior to sweeping dead wood are counted as pins down.

2. If when rolling at a full setup or in order to make a spare, it is discovered immediately after the ball has been delivered that one or more pins are improperly set, although not missing, the ball and resulting pinfall shall be counted. It is each player's responsibility to determine if the setup is correct. He shall insist that any pins incorrectly set be respotted before delivering his ball, otherwise he implies that the setup is satisfactory. No change in the position of any pins which are left standing can be made after a previous delivery in order to make a spare, unless the pin setter has moved or misplaced any pin after the previous delivery and prior to the bowling of the next ball.

140 BOWLING FOR EVERYONE

3. Pins which are knocked down by a fair ball, and remain lying on the lane or in the gutters, or which lean so as to touch kickbacks or side partitions, are termed dead wood and counted as pins down, and must be removed before the next ball is bowled.

Pinfall—Illegal

Rule 9. When any of the following incidents occur the ball counts as a ball rolled, but pins knocked down shall not count:

1. When pins are knocked down or displaced by a ball which leaves the lane before reaching the pins.

2. When a ball rebounds from the rear cushion.

3. When pins come in contact with the body, arms or legs of a human pinsetter and rebound.

4. A standing pin which falls when it is touched by mechanical pinsetting equipment, or when dead wood is removed, or is knocked down by a human pinsetter, shall not count and must be replaced on the pin spot inscribed on the pin deck where it originally stood before delivery of the ball.

5. Pins which are bowled off the lane, rebound, and remain standing on the lane must be counted as pins standing.

6. If in delivering the ball a foul is committed, any pins knocked down by such delivery shall not be counted.

Dead Ball

Rule 10. A ball shall be declared dead if any of the following occur, in which case such ball shall not count. The pins must be respotted after the cause for declaring such dead ball has been removed and player shall be required to rebowl.

a. If, after the player delivers his ball and attention is immediately called to the fact that one or more pins were missing from the setup.

b. When a human pinsetter removes or interferes with any pin or pins before they stop rolling or before the ball reaches the pins.

c. When a player bowls on the wrong lane or out of turn.

d. When a player is interfered with by a pinsetter, another bowler, spectator, or moving object as the ball is being delivered and before delivery is completed, player must then and there accept the resulting pinfall or demand that pins be respotted.

e. When any pins at which he is bowling are moved or knocked

Appendix

down in any manner, as the player is delivering the ball and before the ball reaches the pins.

f. When a player's ball comes in contact with any foreign obstacle.

No Pins May Be Conceded

Rule 11. No pins may be conceded and only those actually knocked down or moved entirely off the playing surface of the lane as a result of the legal delivery of the ball by the player may be counted. Every frame must be completed at the time the player is bowling in his regular order.

Replacement of Pins

Rule 12. Should a pin be broken or otherwise badly damaged during the game, it shall be replaced at once by another as nearly uniform in weight and condition as possible with the set in use. The league or tournament officials shall in all cases be the judges in the matter of replacement of such pins.

A broken pin does not change the score made by a bowler. The number of pins knocked down are counted, after which the broken pin is replaced.

Bowling on Wrong Lane

Rule 13. When only one player or the lead-off men on both teams bowl on the wrong lane and the error is discovered before another player has bowled, a dead ball shall be declared and the player(s) required to rebowl on the correct lane(s).

When more than one player on the same team has bowled on the wrong lane, the game shall be completed without adjustment and the next game shall be started on the correctly scheduled lane.

In singles match play competition, where a player normally bowls two frames each time it is his turn to bowl, and a player bowls on the wrong lane for these two frames, a dead ball shall be declared and the player required to rebowl both frames on the correct lanes providing the error is discovered prior to the time the opposing player has made a legal delivery. If the error is not discovered until the opposing player has bowled, the score shall count and the player shall be required to bowl his subsequent frames on the correct lanes.

142   BOWLING FOR EVERYONE

Balls—Private Ownership

Rule 14. Bowling balls used in the game and marked by their owners are considered private and other participants in the game are prohibited from using the same, unless the owner consents to such use.

Foul—Definition of

Rule 15. A foul is committed with no pinfall being credited to the player although the ball counts as a ball rolled, when a part of the bowler's person encroaches upon or goes beyond the foul line and touches any part of the lane, equipment or building during or after executing a legal delivery. A ball is in play and a foul may be called after legal delivery has been made and until the same or another player is on the approach in position to make a succeeding delivery.

If the player commits a foul which is apparent to both captains or one or more members of each of the opposing teams competing in a league or tournament on the same pair of lanes where the foul is committed, or to the official scorer or a tournament official, and should the foul judge or umpire through negligence fail to see it committed or an ABC approved automatic foul detecting device fails to record it, a foul shall nevertheless be declared and so recorded.

Deliberate Foul

Rule 16. If a player deliberately fouls to benefit by the calling of a foul, he shall be immediately disqualified from further participation in the series then in play and his place may be taken by another player. The deliberate foul shall not be allowed.

A player who willfully throws his ball into the gutter shall be immediately removed from the game and series and his place may be taken by another player.

If no substitute is available to take the place of the removed player, his team shall be credited only with the pins knocked down up to the time the player was disqualified plus one-tenth of his blind score for each of the remaining frames in the game.

Foul Counts as Ball Bowled

Rule 17. A foul ball shall be recorded as a ball bowled by the player, but any pins bowled down when a foul is committed shall not count. When the player fouls upon delivering the first ball of a frame, all pins knocked down must be respotted, and only those pins knocked down by the second ball may be counted. If he bowls down all the pins with his second ball after fouling with the first, it shall be scored as a spare. When less than ten pins are bowled down on the second ball after fouling on the first, it shall be scored as an error. A player who fouls when delivering his second ball of a frame shall be credited with only those pins bowled down with his first ball, provided no foul was committed when the first ball was delivered. When a bowler fouls during the delivery of his first ball in the tenth frame and bowls down all ten pins with his second ball (making a spare) he bowls a third ball and is credited with a spare plus the pins bowled down with the third ball. When a player fouls while delivering his third ball in the tenth frame, only those pins bowled down in delivering his first two balls shall be counted.

Other Foul Line Points
Rule 18. Wherever it is deemed necessary to determine fouls, the officials of any local association, upon authorization by their Board of Directors, may require that a foul line be plainly painted on the walls, posts, division boards, or any other structure in a bowling establishment at any point on a line with the regular foul line.

Protests—Provisional Ball
Rule 19. When a protest involving a foul or the legality of pinfall is entered and it cannot immediately be resolved between the two team captains, a provisional ball or frame shall be bowled by the contestant.

If the protest occurs on the first delivery in a frame, the player shall complete his frame and then bowl another complete frame immediately, unless it involves a question of whether a bowler should receive credit for a strike or a lesser number of pins on his first delivery. In such event, the pin or pins which were protested as constituting illegal pinfall shall be respotted and the player required to bowl another ball.

When the protest occurs on the second delivery, the player shall bowl a provisional ball against the same setup of pins which were standing at the time except when the protest involves a foul in which case no provisional ball shall be necessary.

A record of both scores for the frame in which the provisional delivery was made shall be maintained and the protest referred to the league's Board of Directors or the tournament's managing committee for decision. If unable to reach a decision, the local association or the Congress can be asked for a decision upon submission of all the facts relating to the protest.

No Unreasonable Delay
Rule 20. The league or tournament officials shall allow no unreasonable delay in the progress of any game. Should any member or team participating in a league or tournament refuse to proceed with the game after being directed to do so by the proper authorities, such game or series shall be declared forfeited.

Foul—Detection
Rule 21. League and tournament officials may adopt and use any ABC-approved automatic foul detecting device and where none is available a foul judge must be stationed so he has an unobstructed view of the foul line.

Foul—Appeal
Rule 22. No appeal shall be allowed when a foul is indicated by an approved automatic foul detecting device or is called by a foul judge except when it is proved that the device is not operating properly, or there is a preponderance of evidence that the bowler did not foul.

If the device becomes temporarily inoperative the following procedures shall be used in calling fouls:

1. In tournament play, the tournament management shall assign a human foul judge or arrange for the official scorers to call fouls.
2. In league play, the opposing captains shall call fouls or designate someone to act as a foul judge.

Failure to have the automatic foul detecting device in operation or provide for foul line observance when it is inoperative shall disqualify scores bowled for ABC high score consideration.

Average—Definition of
Rule 23. A bowling average is determined by dividing the total

number of pins credited to a bowler by the number of games bowled in one sanctioned league in a season.

Composite Average—The average of all sanctioned leagues when a player bowls in two or more leagues. This average is determined by adding the total pins for all leagues and dividing the result by the total number of games bowled in all leagues.

Highest Average—The best average in one of several leagues in which a player competes.

When establishing an average in league play, a right-handed bowler must bowl right-handed at all times. Similarly, a left-handed bowler must bowl left-handed at all times. Penalty, forfeiture of game.

No combination of scores bowled both right- and left-handed shall be used in computing an average.

A new average must be established if the bowler finds it necessary to change his delivery from right- to left-handed or vice versa.

In all cases, extra pins or fractions must be disregarded when using averages for handicapping or classification purposes. The extra pins shall be reduced to a percentage of a pin only for the purpose of deciding individual position standings in a league.

Prizes—Proprietors and Their Employees

Rule 24. When a sanctioned tournament is sponsored by the management of a bowling center and the scheduled games are bowled solely in that establishment, the owner or employees of the center shall be ineligible to receive individual or all events prizes unless the tournament rules specifically provide otherwise. This shall not apply in annual championships tournaments of local and state associations.

All other tournaments and leagues may, by rule, restrict the owner of the bowling establishment or his employees from qualifying for individual or all events prizes when the games of the league or tournament are bowled solely in the establishments with which they are associated.

Rule 25. No present rule.

Penalty for Unfair Tactics

Rule 26. Any member of the American Bowling Congress violating the provisions of this rule as outlined below shall be liable for the

BOWLING FOR EVERYONE

penalties indicated, and anyone who is not a member of the Congress but who has violated the provisions of this rule shall be refused membership in the Congress until the Board of Directors of the Congress approves his application.

   a. Attempting to gain an unfair advantage.

      (1) By directly or indirectly tampering with lanes, bowling pins and/or bowling balls so they no longer meet ABC specifications.

      (2) By misrepresenting an average either to gain a greater handicap, or qualify for a lower classification in a league or tournament.

      (3) By establishing an average below his ability and thereby gaining an unfair advantage in handicap or classified competition.

Penalty—Loss of game or games including prize winnings and/or suspension of membership where unfair advantage was secured.

   b. Placing the game of tenpins in jeopardy of unfair criticism by the use of dishonest or disreputable tactics in connection with the game of bowling. Penalty—suspension of membership.

   c. Failing to distribute team prize money in accordance with verbal or written agreements. Penalty—suspension of membership.

   d. Failing to pay fees due for participation in a sanctioned league or tournament. Penalty—suspension of membership.

Rerating Requirements

Rule 27. A bowler whose sanctioned high league average is under 190 shall submit himself for rerating and shall be rerated before entering a sanctioned classified or handicap tournament.

   a. When his accumulated average of not less than twenty-one tournament games during the immediately preceding twelve month period exceeds his high league average by ten or more pins, or

   b. When he has exceeded his high league average by fifteen or more pins in each of five tournaments, i.e., forty-five pins in a three game series, sixty pins in a four game series, etc.—based only on his high series in each of the five tournaments—during the immediately preceding twelve month period.

A bowler who must submit to rerating under a. and/or b. shall be responsible to present in writing the names of, and his scores and known prize winnings in all tournaments in which he has competed in the previous twelve months, including those still running:

c. To the tournament manager at least one hour prior to participation in the tournament; rerating by the tournament manager shall establish the bowler's entering average for that tournament only, or

d. To his local association; rerating by the local association (in accordance with the second paragraph, Article 8, Section 4 of the Local Association Constitution) shall establish the bowler's official average and shall be used as his entering average in subsequent tournaments unless he establishes a higher league average or exceeds the rerated average in the manner set forth in a. or b. herein, in which case he must submit for further rerating in accordance with this rule. The rerate (number of pins added to the bowler's average) under c. or d. shall be

e. 80 per cent of the difference by which the bowler's highest league average in such preceding twelve months is exceeded by his tournament average established by reason of a. except that the rerated average may not succeed 200.

f. 50 per cent of the difference by which the bowlers highest league average in such preceding 12 months is exceeded by his tournament average or 200, whichever is lower, established by reason of b.

Where both e. and f. apply the higher rerated average shall be used.

Failure to submit for rerating when required in accordance with the foregoing shall cause the forfeiture of all entry fees and all prize winnings for that and any subsequent tournament for which the bowler did not submit to rerating in accordance with this rule, and shall make him liable for suspension from membership in ABC.

Nothing in this rule will be deemed to supersede the authority of a tournament manager or local association to rerate a bowler who does not exceed his entering average by reason of a. or b.

Penalty—Libel or Slander
Rule 28. A bowler who libels or utters slanderous accusations against an official or officials, member or members of an association, league or team affiliated with the American Bowling Congress, which cannot be substantiated by sworn facts in the case, shall be deemed unworthy of retaining membership in the ABC.

148 BOWLING FOR EVERYONE

Using Assumed Name
Rule 29. a. No person shall bowl under an assumed name or bowl under the name of another person scheduled to bowl in any sanctioned league or tournament.

Penalty—Forfeiture of all games in which such a player was used and all involved and found guilty shall be liable for suspension of membership.

Suspended Bowler Ineligible
Rule 29. b. When a bowler is suspended from or denied membership in ABC he shall be ineligible to bowl or pace in any sanctioned league or tournament until reinstated by ABC.

Penalty—When a team knowingly uses a suspended bowler it shall forfeit all games in which the suspended player was used and all involved found guilty shall be liable for suspension from membership.

Penalty—Fund Shortages
Rule 30. a. When an officer of a sanctioned league, ABC or American Junior Bowling Congress, chartered local or state association embezzles, defalcates or absconds with any funds entrusted to him, he shall be liable for indefinite suspension from membership in the Congress.

b. The officer required to make monthly verifications of the accounts of such organizations may also be liable for indefinite suspension from membership if he has been guilty of malfeasance or nonfeasance in performing this duty.

c. When an officer or officers of a sanctioned league, chartered local or state association that has suffered a loss, deliberately make or file false statements with the bonding company in order to collect a larger sum than that to which the league, state or local association would be entitled to under the bond, they shall be liable for suspension from membership in the ABC.

Procedures for Suspension Action
Rule 31. When the Executive Secretary-Treasurer of the American Bowling Congress is advised, after appropriate investigation, that a member who is covered under the ABC bonding program has been

Appendix 149

guilty of acts within the meaning of Sections a. or b. or both of Rule 30, he shall cause the following action to be instituted.

1. Notify the person or persons that suspension charges are being preferred and the reason therefor.
2. Such notification shall be sent by Registered or Certified Mail and shall specifically state the cause of the action and outline the time and method for filing an appeal.
3. Notification of the action shall be filed with the local association secretary and also appropriate league or tournament officials.
4. Submit a report and his findings to the ABC Legal Committee.

Reinstatement of membership in all cases where a suspension is imposed shall be available only upon written application to and approval by the Board of Directors of the Congress, or an appropriate committee of its members authorized to act on such application for reinstatement of membership.

Protests—Time Limit
Rule 32. Protests involving eligibility, scoring or general playing rules in sanctioned leagues and tournaments shall be governed as follows:

Leagues Any protest affecting eligibility or general playing rules must be confirmed in writing to a responsible league or local association official or the American Bowling Congress not later than fifteen (15) days after the series in which the infraction occurred has been bowled. If no written protest is entered prior to the expiration of the fifteen-day period, the series must stand as bowled. Protests resulting out of competition in the final two weeks of a league's schedule must be filed within forty-eight hours of the concluding night of the league schedule.

Tournaments Any protest affecting eligibility or general playing rules must be confirmed in writing to a responsible tournament or local association official or to the American Bowling Congress before the tournament prize payments are made.

Obvious Errors Errors in scoring or errors in calculation in league or tournament play must be corrected by a responsible league or tournament official immediately upon discovery of such error. Questionable errors shall be decided upon by the league's Board of Directors or the managing committee of the tournament. The managing committee of a tournament may, by rule, set a time limit for correction of errors.

Each protest under this rule must be specific in itself and this rule shall not be construed to cover a previous or similar violation.

Gambling—Pool—Lottery
Rule 33. No bowling proprietor shall allow on his premises handbooks, pools or any schemes of a gambling nature to be made or handled involving the outcome of bowling games, whether the bowling games be sanctioned league or tournament play. Failure to terminate such gambling practices in his establishments, or any part thereof, when such practices are within his knowledge, or when he shall have been notified of same shall be cause for such violations being called to the attention of the local association officers.

The following procedure is then mandatory:

1. The local association shall immediately call a meeting of the Board of Directors of this association.

2. Upon due proof being submitted to the Board that such proprietor is in violation of the tenets of this section, and that such proprietor has knowledge of this condition, it shall be the duty of said officials to order such bowling proprietor to immediately cease, or cause to be terminated, such gambling practices.

3. Upon such proprietor's refusal to obey this order, said local association officials shall notify secretaries of all sanctioned leagues bowling in such proprietor's establishment, or establishments, that said proprietor is in violation of American Bowling Congress laws.

4. Upon the bowling proprietor's refusal to obey such order, the local association officials shall recommend to the American Bowling Congress that said bowling proprietor's lane certification be cancelled immediately, and the sanctions of all leagues which continue to bowl in said proprietor's establishment, or establishments, be withdrawn.

Teams and individual entries representing names of gambling individuals, corporations, or syndicates, or of gambling devices, shall not be accepted by the American Bowling Congress.

Any American Bowling Congress member found to be participating in or actively engaged in the management of any schemes within the meaning of the gambling activity outlined in paragraph one of this section shall upon his refusal to discontinue such practices after having been notified by the officials of the local association, be reported to the American Bowling Congress with the recommendation that he be suspended from membership in the ABC.

Supplemental Fee
Rule 34. Members of the American Bowling Congress may not participate in or operate any pool, lottery or any gambling scheme or arrangement where the scores bowled in sanctioned league or tournament play, partially or otherwise, are used to determine the prize winners. In addition, no member of the ABC shall pay a supplemental fee of any type or character for the purpose of having his sanctioned league or tournament score or scores qualify for prizes outside the specific league or tournament in which the score was bowled except as provided in this rule for charity purposes.

The penalty for a violation of this rule both for the participants and promoters shall be suspension from ABC membership.

Scores bowled in sanctioned league play may be used to determine prize winners in a supplementary contest when the following conditions are observed:

1. A minimum of two-thirds of the gross collected as entry fees must be donated to a recognized charitable organization.
2. Entry may be made available to all bowlers in a single local association and its metropolitan area.
3. The maximum entry fee shall not exceed $2 per person.
4. Operating costs shall in no case exceed ten cents (10¢) per person.
5. The local association under whose jurisdiction the event is held shall be represented officially on the managing or operating committee.
6. The Board of Directors of the local association shall be authorized to withhold approval of events as described herein when any organization or organizations sharing in the proceeds are not bona fide charitable organizations.

152   BOWLING FOR EVERYONE

Approaches—Must Not be Defaced
Rule 35. No one shall mark on or shall introduce on any part of the approach or lane any substance which will have a tendency to injure, disfigure or place the approach or lane in such condition as to detract from the possibility of other bowlers being able to take advantage of the usual conditions. The use of such substances as aristol, talcum powder, pumice, resin, etc., on shoes; the use of soft rubber soles and heels that rub off, and in any manner alter the normal condition of the approach, are strictly prohibited.

Automatic Scoring Devices
Rule 36. An automatic scoring device which has been approved by the ABC Board of Directors may be used in sanctioned league and tournament play.

This device shall provide a printed record of the score which can be audited frame by frame and otherwise comply with the scoring and playing rules of the game.

Appearance at Suspension Hearing
Rule 37. When a member(s) of the American Bowling Congress files charges against another member(s) and fails to appear without sufficient cause to testify at a hearing on the case conducted by an association or a special ABC Investigations Committee, such ABC member(s) shall be liable for suspension from ABC membership.

Temporary Suspension of an Officer
Rule 38. When charges of misappropriation or mishandling of funds or a bond claim has been filed against an association or league officer, the association and/or league shall temporarily suspend the officer from all offices held until the matter has been considered by the ABC Legal Committee. In the interim, another officer shall be appointed to perform the duties of the officer who is under temporary suspension.

This procedure shall apply in all such cases except where an appeal is made to the ABC Executive Secretary-Treasurer who may at his discretion authorize the officer to resume his duties pending Legal Committee action.

Appendix 153

In the meantime, the member shall continue to be eligible to bowl in ABC sanctioned competition.

High Score Awards

Competitive Team Awards

Rule 50. The Congress shall prepare and present appropriate plaques to the sponsors of two-, three-, four-, and five-man teams who bowl the high three fiscal year scores in each of the following classifications:

Three game series total.
Single team game scores.

Individual Awards (1 Game)

Rule 51. The Congress shall prepare and present suitably engraved awards, approved as official by the Board of Directors of the Congress, to any duly qualified member of the Congress in good standing who shall, in any single game in sanctioned league or tournament play anywhere under the jurisdiction of the Congress, have attained the scores of 300, 299, 298.

Individual Awards (3 Game)

Rule 52. The Congress shall present suitably engraved awards to the members who bowl one of the three highest scores in a three-game series in sanctioned league or tournament play under its jurisdiction during each fiscal year ending July 31.

No individual shall be entitled to receive more than one fiscal year award for high three-game series totals. An individual qualifying more than once shall receive recognition only for the highest series bowled by him.

Award of Merit

Rule 53. The Congress shall present an Award of Merit to the bowlers in each local association who have bowled the highest single game and the highest three-game total in sanctioned league or tournament play under the following conditions:

1. The game or series was bowled by a member of the association in an establishment within the jurisdiction of the association.
2. The final average sheet or the average sheet as of a date requested by the association is filed with the association secretary.
3. The award shall be based on the scores rolled between August 1 and July 31, except those associations which publish average books may adopt a specific date for determining award winners providing scores bowled thereafter are counted in the next season's competition.
4. Duplicate awards shall be presented in case of ties.

The single-game award of merit shall only be provided in such local associations when no member thereof has during the same season, or within the dates set by the association, bowled a high score of 300, 299 or 298 which has or will receive ABC high score recognition. No claim will receive consideration if submitted later than thirty days after the close of the bowling season in which the score was bowled.

EDITOR'S NOTE
Where the same local association member bowled the highest single game and highest three-game series, he will receive only one award which will be engraved to carry the high single and high three-game scores.

Special Awards
Rule 54. The Congress shall present to qualified members awards in recognition of the following special accomplishments:

For bowling eleven strikes in a row in a game where the score is 297 or less.
For converting the 7-10 split.
For converting the 4-6-7-10 split.
For bowling three consecutive games of the same score in a series.
For bowling a three-game series totaling 700 to 799.
For bowling 800 or better in a three-game series.
For bowling one hundred pins over average providing the bowler's score does not qualify him for another ABC high-game award.
The following shall apply to averages on which winners are deter-

Appendix 155

mined in qualifying for the Century Award (one hundred pins over average).

League Play

Last season's average (minimum of twenty-one games) in the same league for the first twenty-one games.

Last season's highest average (minimum of twenty-one games) for new members of the league for the first twenty-one games.

After a current 21-game average is established, current average shall apply. A bowler with no 21-game average for the previous season becomes eligible after establishing a 21-game current average.

Tournament Play

In handicap or classified tournaments, the average used in the tournament.

In scratch tournaments, the bowler's highest current average (minimum of twenty-one games).

If no current average of twenty-one or more games, the highest previous season's average (minimum of twenty-one games).

These awards shall be subject to the requirements for regular ABC High Score Awards as defined in Rule 56 herein, with the exception of the requirements for weighing pins, measuring the lanes, and the procedure for filing notification that a bowler has qualified for an award.

Claims for such special awards shall be on a form or forms prepared by the Executive Secretary-Treasurer of the American Bowling Congress, and must be filed as directed on the application form for the award.

Series Awards—More than 3 Games

Rule 55. When more than three games are bowled in a series, only the first three games shall count for ABC three-game series awards. However, if six or more games are bowled in a series each succeeding set of three games, following the first three games, shall qualify for ABC three-game series awards. In match game or elimination tournaments where less than three games in a series are bowled against the same opponent the games shall not qualify for ABC three-game series awards.

156 BOWLING FOR EVERYONE

The provisions of this rule shall also apply to play-offs for ties in leagues and tournaments.

Conditions Governing Awards

Rule 56. The following are the requirements which must be met for eligibility for ABC high score awards:

1. The high score must have been bowled in a league or tournament sanctioned by the American Bowling Congress.

2. The lanes upon which the score was bowled must have been certified by the American Bowling Congress for the current season prior to the bowling of the high score game.

3. A competent foul judge or an automatic foul detecting device approved by the American Bowling Congress must have been employed during the full time the score was being bowled.

4. Every provision of the ABC constitution, rules and regulations must have been in effect by those conducting the league or tournament in which the high score was bowled.

5. Notification of the high score must be given to the local association secretary within 24 hours after it has been bowled. This notification must be given by the league or tournament secretary.

6. No more than fourteen (14) days may elapse before the local association secretary or president gives such notification to the Executive Secretary-Treasurer of the American Bowling Congress.

7. The secretary of the local association or his duly authorized representative must inspect and measure the lanes on which the score was bowled, and inspect and weigh the very pins used when the high score was bowled. These pins should be set aside in a receptacle immediately after conclusion of the series and sealed in the presence of the two opposing team captains awaiting their inspection and weighing by the local association secretary or his duly authorized representative. This inspection and weighing together with the examination of the lanes must be done within seventy-two hours after the score has been rolled. He must submit his completed report or affidavit to the American Bowling Congress, setting forth his recommendation for approval or rejection of the claim. The report signed by opposing captains or players, foul judge, official scorer, league or tournament secretary, together with the original score sheet, or a true

Appendix 157

copy of the original score sheet, must reach the office of the American Bowling Congress before thirty days have elapsed.

8. When claims for recognition of individual high games of 300, 299, and 298 are submitted, the Executive Secretary-Treasurer of the American Bowling Congress may approve the issuance of the award immediately upon receipt of the evidence and affidavits required, or he may refer claims to the ABC Board of Directors and delegates for their consideration.